Rolls-Royce Car, number 925,

afternoon the complete ascent

Funicular Railway negotiating

to the top, without reversing

The Car was driven by the

ard throughout the performance.

a Car of this wheel-base has

t reversing.

th of March, 1909.

Correspondent "Daily Telegraph."

'91

Merry
Christmas,
David!
Have you seen the new
Rolls-Royce Golf Cart?
Gary and Darlene

GREAT MARQUES
ROLLS-ROYCE

GREAT MARQUES
ROLLS-ROYCE

JONATHAN WOOD

GENERAL EDITOR
JOHN BLUNSDEN

CHARTWELL
BOOKS, INC.

This edition 1989

**Published by Chartwell Books, Inc.
A division of Book Sales, Inc.
110 Enterprise Avenue
Secaucus, New Jersey 07094**

© Octopus Books Ltd 1982

ISBN: 1-55521-419-3

Produced by Mandarin Offset
Printed and bound in Hong Kong

ENDPAPERS *The manoeuvrability
of the Silver Ghost model displayed
to effect in a climb of the steep and
twisting Hermitage Road, Nice, in
1909, with Rolls himself at the
wheel. This series of photographs
and testimony were used by
Rolls-Royce as publicity material
in 1910.*

PAGES 1-5 *The latest Rolls-Royce –
the Silver Spirit. Provided by
Rolls-Royce Motors Limited.*

Author's note

I have much enjoyed writing this book. Rolls-Royce is, after all, a unique automotive institution and its history has a fascination all of its own. But no book can be written without help, and first and foremost my thanks must go to the Rolls-Royce Enthusiasts' Club and its Secretary, Lieutenant-Colonel Eric Barrass OBE, and of course those club members who allowed their magnificent cars to be photographed.

On the other side of the Atlantic, Bob and June Barrymore, of La Jolla, California, went to enormous lengths to ensure that we could photograph a superb cross-section of Rolls-Royces in California, and our grateful thanks to them and those owners who provided their cars for photography. (Owners and custodians of all the cars, at the time of photography, are given in the captions.) Also, we would like to thank Kenneth B. Gooding and his staff at the Merle Norman Classic Beauty Collection in Sylmar, California, for their help and assistance.

We have received the utmost cooperation from Rolls-Royce Motors and in particular I would like to thank Dennis Miller-Williams, Public Relations Manager at Conduit Street, for his help.

Also my thanks must go to *Autocar* magazine and Warren Allport for providing so many of the performance figures used within these pages.

Finally, I would like to thank Ian Dawson and Chris Linton who took the majority of the splendid photographs.

Jonathan Wood

Reproduction of Rolls-Royce Trademarks and Copyright material is made with the kind permission of its owners

Special photography: **Ian Dawson and Chris Linton**

CONTENTS

THE
MANCHESTER
MEETING

Early in May 1904 three businessmen sat down to lunch at Manchester's newly opened Midland Hotel to discuss motor cars. The Midland has no doubt witnessed many such commercial meetings but this one triggered a chain of events that was to create the most illustrious of all names to be associated with the automobile. For, as a result, Rolls-Royce Ltd was established.

At first sight Rolls and Royce must have made unlikely dining companions. Frederick Henry Royce, who was 41 at the time, was a miller's son and largely self-taught, and had achieved commercial success in the face of overwhelming personal odds. By contrast, at 26 years of age, the Hon. Charles Stewart Rolls, a peer's son, had followed an assured aristocratic path to Eton and Trinity College, Cambridge, and was supported, to some extent, by a wealthy father. The final member of the luncheon party was Henry Edmunds, who knew both men and had effected the meeting. His catalytic role must surely make him godfather of the Rolls/Royce alliance. To find out how this historic meeting came to take place, and what drew the two principal characters into the same unlikely orbit, we must examine the respective careers of Royce and Rolls and the times in which they lived.

Henry Royce

Frederick Henry Royce was born on 27 March 1863. His father, James Royce, described himself as a 'farmer and miller' on his marriage to Mary King. That took place in 1852 at Woodham Ferrers, Essex, which was Mary's home. In all, five children were born to the couple, Henry being the youngest. But by the time of his birth the family had moved to Alwalton, near Peterborough, where James managed mills for the Ecclesiastical Commissioners, the body concerned with Church of England properties and stipends. History has cast James Royce as a shadowy, luckless figure but it should be remembered that agriculture was in a state of decline at the time, so how much was due to circumstances or personality is difficult to establish. What we do know is that James took Henry and his other son, also called James, with him when he left the quiet banks of the River Nene for the bustling, friendless streets of London in the hope of obtaining work. Meanwhile his wife and daughters remained in Alwalton. The year was 1867 and Henry was four, but James Royce seems to have had as little success in London as he did in rural Lincolnshire. Ill fortune seemed to haunt the man for he died in 1872 at the early age of 41. This left nine-year-old Henry faced with the task of getting work for himself. For a time he sold newspapers for W. H. Smith and, at the age of ten, he became a telegraph boy in London's opulent West End. By all accounts Mary Royce did her best for her youngest but she seemed to have been ill-equipped for early widowhood. In later life Henry spoke little of his early years, but he did tell a close friend that at this time his food for the day was 'often but two slices of bread soaked in milk'.

Fortunately help was at hand, for his aunt had a little money and Henry's mechanical aptitudes were clearly developing because she managed to secure a £20-a-year apprenticeship for him at the Great Northern Railway Works at Peterborough, only a few miles from his birthplace. He was 14 at the time and he later recalled that there 'I acquired some skill as a mechanic but lacked technical, commercial and clerical experience.' The three years spent with the Great Northern instilled some stability in his all too insecure and unhappy life. Apart from benefiting from mechanical skills, he embarked on a bout of self-education, teaching himself those subjects he had missed when his energies were geared to survival. Elementary education, it should be remembered, did not become compulsory in England until 1888. So he sharpened up his mathematics and learned algebra, and began teaching himself the rudiments of the new power source that had clearly captured his imagination: electricity. By good chance the owner of his lodging, a Mr Yarrow, had a lathe in his garden shed, along with a carpenter's bench, shaping machine and grinder, tools that Henry was able to use to develop his extraordinary skills in the working and shaping of metals.

Then, tragically, fate again intervened and his aunt found herself unable to continue payments for his apprenticeship. So, in 1879, he was again looking for work. He travelled north to Leeds where he worked for a firm of machine-tool makers who paid him 11 shillings for a 54-hour week. Later he was to remember starting work at 6 am and finishing at 10 pm for months on end. Then, by chance, he saw an advertisement for a tester with the London-based Electric Light and Power Company, which had acquired the patents and services of that versatile American inventor, Hiram P. Maxim. Royce got the job and moved back to

London, taking lodgings in Kentish Town. He continued his self-education by night, also attending Professor William Ayrton's evening classes and other lectures at the Polytechnic in Regent Street.

Royce's ability and dedication must have made a good impression on his employers for in 1882, at the age of 19, he was sent to Liverpool to manage the firm's affairs in that city. His responsibilities included the supervision of the then somewhat precarious business of theatrical electric lighting, but his employment with the Lancashire Maxim and Western Electric Company was destined to be shortlived for the enterprise foundered.

Henry, however, had struck up a friendship with another young electrical engineer, a London doctor's son named Ernest Claremont. In 1884, when Royce was 21 and on a modest capital of £70 (Claremont contributed £50 and Royce, incredibly, £20) they set up an electrical business, renting a small room in Cooke Street, off Stretford Road in Manchester. In the first instance F. H. Royce and Co. produced lampholders, progressing to bells and eventually dynamos. It was these dynamos that gave Royce an opportunity to express his perfectionist ideals. He quickly grasped the importance of producing a unit with a sparkless commutator, thus eliminating a potential fire hazard: a crucial factor for any establishment installing a generating set, but particularly on board ship, or in a paper or cotton mill. Although trade fluctuated, and competition from America and Germany was an ever-present challenge, Royce and Claremont worked long hours and gradually their efforts were rewarded.

These factors of improved circumstances and stability, the first he had ever enjoyed, were no doubt considerations when in 1893, at the age of 30, Henry Royce married. His bride was Minnie, the daughter of Alfred Punt, a London printer; rather conveniently, Claremont married the other sister. F. H. Royce and Co also benefited, for Punt put money into the firm.

By 1894, just ten years after its inception, the business had grown sufficiently to become a public company and there was a change of name to Royce Ltd. Then the invention of the electric crane lent itself perfectly to Royce improvement and refinement, and soon attained a worldwide reputation for the company. By 1899 orders stood at an impressive £20,000. A works and foundry were established at Trafford Park, Manchester, which was Britain's first industrial estate. Royce's growing prosperity was apparent when he and his wife, along with Minnie's adopted niece Violet, moved into a specially built house in fashionable Legh Road, Knutsford, designed by none other than the architect of Manchester Town Hall, Alfred Waterhouse.

We should, perhaps, pause here to consider the birth and appearance of the motor car, which by the turn of the century was beginning to make its presence felt on Britain's roads. It was in 1885 that Karl Benz and Gottlieb Daimler, working quite independently of each other in Germany, had created self-propelled carriages powered by internal combustion engines that were saleable to the general public. The

French were soon to take up the idea while the British, who clearly represented the most prosperous European market of the day, had to import vehicles from the Continent before their own industry got on a sound footing.

So when Henry Royce acquired his first horseless carriage it is no surprise to find that it was a French De Dion Bouton Quadricycle. Claremont and their friend and doctor H. Campbell-Thompson acquired similar machines. It was hoped that Royce, with the leafy lanes of Cheshire and Derbyshire now within easy reach, would lessen his work load. Maybe he was driven by the fear that those terrible, poverty-stricken days would one day return but his health, which had inevitably suffered during the privations of his youth, was never robust. So Campbell-Thompson suggested a break and, in 1902, Henry at last agreed and went on a ten-week cruise to South Africa with his wife, who had relatives there. On his return his doctor again took a hand, suggesting that Henry, to avoid over-exerting himself, should buy a motor car. Therefore a second-hand 1901 French Decauville was acquired. The arrival of the Royce car was drawing ever nearer.

PRECEDING PAGES The two-cylinder 10 hp engine of the earliest surviving Rolls-Royce of 1904. Provided by T. and E. Love.

ABOVE The Hon. Charles Stewart Rolls (1877-1910), third son of Lord Llangattock, who died at the age of 32, the first Englishman to die in a flying accident.

ABOVE RIGHT Sir Henry Royce (1863-1933), self-taught genius who Rolls regarded as 'the world's greatest motor engineer'. He was created a baronet in 1930.

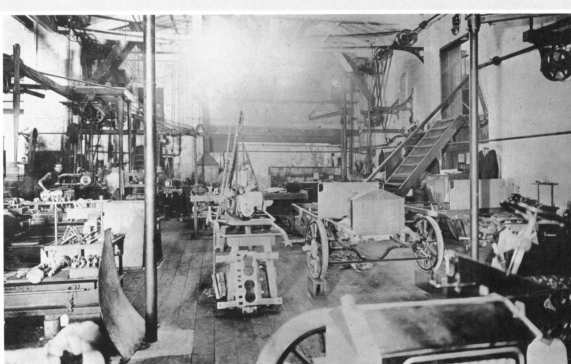

ABOVE Royce Limited's cramped premises at Cooke Street, Manchester. A two-cylinder car is in the foreground with two four-cylinder cars positioned centrally; a crankcase for the latter can clearly be seen leaning against the chassis. The stairs on the right lead to the offices of Royce, company secretary John de Looze and to the drawing office and instrument room.

LEFT Chassis of the first 10 hp Royce car, though lacking a fan and before the fitting of a four-seater body. Surely it was this photograph that convinced Rolls of the need to travel to Manchester to meet Royce? For the precision and clarity of line bear the hallmark of all Henry Royce's work. Note the rear-driven wheels have more spokes than the front ones: common practice in those days. The famous Classically inspired radiator has yet to appear.

Royce was in for a nasty shock when he went to collect the Decauville, which had been conveyed to Manchester by train. Unfortunately it failed to start and Henry had to undergo the indignity of being pushed back to Cooke Street by four labourers while he sat at the steering wheel giving directions. The car was left in a shed and the following day Royce set about getting it running. As it happened the Decauville was a fairly reputable make and its apocryphal reputation for crudeness and unreliability probably says more about Royce's perfectionist standards than about shortcomings in the 10 hp two-cylinder car from Corbeil. As it happened, Royce's electrical business was not enjoying the buoyancy that had marked its formative years and, with that activity concentrated at Trafford Park, he decided to employ the spare capacity available at Cooke Street to enter the motor business. Doctor Campbell-Thompson's plan for Royce to take things easier by getting a car had gone seriously awry!

Early in 1903 work on the Royce car began. Henry was assisted by mechanic Ernie Mills, who was already acquainted with the works of the Decauville, and two electrical apprentices, Tom Haldenby and Eric Platford. From the very outset of the project, Royce employed light, yet strong, nickel steel for many chassis and engine parts and enough components to build three cars were produced. Royce worked ceaselessly on the project and all too often the instrument room foreman would arrive to start work at 6.30 am only to find his employer slumped over his bench, having worked throughout the night on the car, and then collapsed from sheer exhaustion. Much of the Royce car was actually produced at Cooke Street: the patterns, aluminium and bronze castings were made there, but the iron castings came from the Trafford Park works. Forgings were bought out from the Manchester firm of Mountford Brothers and, naturally, the car's ignition system was designed by Royce himself. A local carriage maker produced a simple four-seater body.

By all accounts the 10 hp two-cylinder 1800 cc Royce performed well enough on its first outing. Naturally Henry took the wheel and drove the car on a 24 km (15 mile) run to his Knutsford home. The second car went to Ernest Claremont, who at first had not been over-enthusiastic about Royce Ltd entering the motor trade. Henry Edmunds, a director of the company, had the third car and he was destined to play a crucial role in the creation of Rolls-Royce Ltd. He acquired his share in the company almost by chance. Edmunds was a director of W. T. Glover and Co, a firm that was also based at Trafford Park and supplied Royce with electrical cables. It so transpired that Claremont decided to take a financial interest in Glover and he acquired shares from Edmunds in exchange for Royce stock. Henry Edmunds, also a pioneer electrical engineer, was a prominent member of the London-based Automobile Club of Great Britain and Ireland (later to become the RAC); a fellow member was the Hon. Charles Rolls, a pioneer motorist and third son of Lord Llangattock of Monmouth.

The Hon. Charles Rolls

Charles Stewart Rolls was born in London on 27 August 1877 though he grew up at The Hendre, the family's Monmouthshire country seat. His father was John Allan Rolls, the grandson of the seventh Earl of Northesk, who became Baron Llangattock in 1892 when Charles was 15. His education began at Mortimer Vicarage School, near Reading, Berkshire, and in 1891 he followed his two brothers to Eton, entering the Rev. H. Daman's house. He was there for only three years, leaving at the end of the Easter Half in 1894 because his father regarded travel as an essential ingredient of his education. Charles seems to have displayed little academic flair though he improved somewhat towards the end of his time at school. What did absorb him were the opportunities presented by electrical power. He had urged his father to adopt electric light at The Hendre and a generating set was duly installed. His enthusiasm for the new power source was such that, on leaving Eton, his housemaster commented, somewhat ruefully, that Charles had decided to make electricity 'his chosen career'. An Army commission had been contemplated, a much more conventional pursuit for a member of the ruling classes, but Charles seems to have been intent on pursuing his electrical bent.

Holidays and the period between leaving Eton and going to university included journeys on the family's steam yacht *Santa Maria,* which took them as far afield as the Crimean battlefields, St Petersburg and even Moscow, an agreeable visiting place for the British aristocracy in those pre-revolutionary days. But far more influential was a trip that Charles made with his parents to Paris in 1894. The French capital was then the automobile centre of the world and the 17-year-old Rolls undoubtedly saw some of the most modern cars of the day jostling with horse-drawn transport on the bustling Parisian streets.

Soon afterwards, Charles entered Trinity College, Cambridge, instead of following his brothers to Oxford, as he wanted to read for an engineering degree. He became an enthusiastic cyclist and in addition to absorbing engineering theory he also gained practical experience. 'I go three times a week to the engineering workshop under Professor Ewing, which is very interesting,' he told his father.

He was also pursuing his fascination for the motor car. Early in 1896 he spent a weekend at Broomhill, the home of Sir David Salomons, near Tunbridge Wells, Kent. As the British motor industry was virtually non-existent at this time, Salomons and his like-minded contemporaries

RIGHT *T. and E. Love's 1904 10 hp car, earliest surviving example of the marque. Chassis number is 20154. (Below: the model displayed in a 1905 catalogue of Rolls-Royce cars.)*

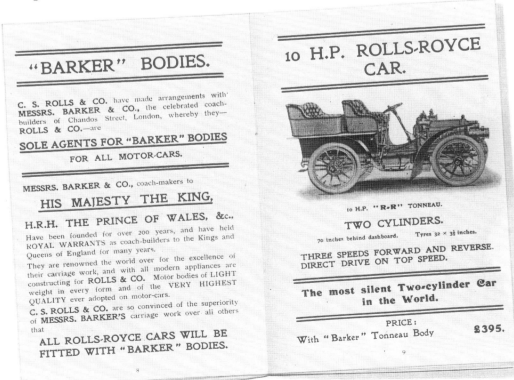

10 hp (1904-6)	
ENGINE	
Type	Cast-iron fixed-head monobloc, on aluminium crankcase
No. of cylinders	2
Bore/stroke mm	95.2 × 127 (later cars 99.8 × 127)
Displacement cc	1800 (2000)
Valve operation	Pushrod overhead inlet; side exhaust
Sparkplugs per cyl.	1
Compression ratio	3:1
Carburation	Royce float feed spray type
BHP	12 at 1000 rpm
DRIVE TRAIN	
Clutch	Cone
Transmission	Separate 3-speed gearbox, via open propeller shaft, to fully floating rear axle
CHASSIS	
Frame	Channel section with gearbox subframe
Wheelbase mm	1905
Track mm	1219
Suspension – front	Half elliptic
Suspension – rear	Half elliptic
Brakes	Rear only. Footbrake operating on transmission; handbrake internal expanding on rear wheels
Tyre size	810 × 90
Wheels	Artillery with wooden spokes
PERFORMANCE	
Maximum speed	61 km/h (38 mph)
Number built	16

had to content themselves with importing cars from the continent of Europe. Sir David had been responsible for initiating the first public display of motor vehicles at Tunbridge Wells the previous year and was an enthusiastic Peugeot owner. It is no surprise to find that later in the year, when Rolls wanted to buy his first car, he went to Paris and brought back a 3¾ hp Peugeot, and no doubt proceeded to raise eyebrows at Cambridge University. The following year he sampled the questionable delights of a De Dion Bouton tricycle and Léon Bollée tri-car but, at the end of 1897, he progressed to a much more powerful machine by buying a 2.4-litre four-cylinder Panhard. This was the actual car that had won the previous year's Paris – Marseille – Paris race and Rolls paid £1200 for it, a goodly sum in those days.

Charles Rolls graduated in 1898 and on leaving Cambridge threw himself wholeheartedly into motoring and the promotion of the car. He was already a member of Sir David Salomons' learned Self Propelled Traffic Association and had been a committee member of the prestigious Automobile Club of Great Britain since November 1897.

He was a regular attender at club gatherings but he probably became known to a wider public in 1900 when he won the club's 1000 Mile Trial. This event, which took competitors from London, west to Bristol and then north to Edinburgh, via Birmingham and Manchester, and back to the capital through York, Leeds and Nottingham, was organized by the club's secretary, Claude Goodman Johnson. The event was destined to put the motor car on a serious footing in Britain and Rolls, at the wheel of a 12 hp Panhard, was awarded the gold medal for the best performance, irrespective of class. This was no mean feat when it is realized that, of the 65 or so entrants, only 35 managed to complete the whole distance under their own power.

The C.S. Rolls and Co. motor agency

Rolls continued to campaign his cars, both at home and abroad, but the next significant event, as far as the Rolls-Royce story is concerned, came in January 1902 when C.S. Rolls and Co. was formed. Charles had gone into business as a motor agent; the capital for the venture came

ABOVE *The second oldest Rolls-Royce, a 1905 15 hp three-cylinder model, sole survivor of the six made and now on show at the Doune Motor Museum, Perthshire, Scotland. First owner was the Hon. Captain T. Dundas of Northallerton, Yorkshire. Now owned by Royal Scottish Automobile Club.*

RIGHT *The short-lived V8-engined Legalimit model as illustrated in the 1906 Rolls-Royce catalogue. It shared the same power unit as the Invisible Engine model. Only three V8s and parts of a fourth were made.*

from his father, who financed his son by an initial payment of £6500 of the £20,000 legacy due on his death. Rolls operated from Lille Hall in Lille Mews, Seagrave Road, in the London district of Fulham. The premises had previously served as a roller-skating rink. There was a hard asphalt floor, with lock-up garages built up around the central arena. Showrooms were later opened in Brook Street in London's West End. Panhards formed the basis of his sales and, although Rolls was an influential and enthusiastic salesman, from late 1903 he was joined by Claude Johnson, who had resigned from the secretaryship of the Automobile Club earlier in the year. Rolls continued to compete in events in Britain and on the Continent, but after a couple of years of trading he began to look around for other marques to promote as Panhard sales were beginning to falter. So he took on the Minerva from Belgium and later was to turn to the British-made New Orleans.

What Rolls, who fostered an intensely patriotic spirit, wanted was to sell a British-built car to rival the better products of France and Germany. But he was disinclined to embark on manufacture himself: 'Firstly on account of my own incompetence and inexperience in such matters and secondly on account of the enormous risks involved, and at the same time I could not come across any English motor car that I really liked.' He was looking for three- or four-cylinder models, having little time for two-cylinder cars.

This is where Henry Edmunds reappears in the story, the director of the Manchester-based Royce Ltd who was also an acquaintance of Rolls. In March 1904 he had clearly told Rolls about the Royce car and suggested that Royce should travel to London to discuss the matter. He then sent Rolls photographs of the two-cylinder Royce. It seems likely that these pictures clinched the matter, persuading Rolls to go to Manchester to see Royce and the car. For on the face of it a two-cylinder prototype built by an unfamiliar Manchester electrical engineer would seem to be an unlikely vehicle to attract Rolls's attention. But anyone looking at the photographs of the 10 hp Royce can only be impressed by the appearance of the vehicle. Even though it is a small car it possesses a precision of line and clear-sighted refinement that is to be found in all Royce's subsequent work. And Rolls, himself a qualified engineer, would have responded instantly to such a design.

So, a little more than a month after the first 10 hp Royce had taken to the road, Rolls and Edmunds left London by train for Manchester early in May 1904. Settled in the dining car as they sped northwards, Edmunds later recalled that Rolls, with remarkable prescience, told him that his ambition was 'to have a motor car connected with his name so that in the future it might be a household word, just as much as Broadwood or Steinway in connection with pianos; or Chubb in connection with safes'.

On arrival in Manchester they met Royce at the Midland Hotel. Edmunds, who later recorded his impressions of the meeting, says that Rolls and Royce 'took to each other at first sight'. For, although they had such contrasting social backgrounds both had practical engineering experience, shared an equal enthusiasm for electricity and both were of

a parsimonious persuasion: Royce no doubt through circumstances, Rolls displaying a family trait. After lunch, Rolls inspected the Royce car and his response to it can be gauged by the fact that on his return to London he dragged Claude Johnson from his bed to inform him, 'I have found the greatest motor engineer in the world.' Unfortunately that very day Johnson had committed C.S. Rolls and Co. to finance a company to produce electric broughams, for which he harboured some personal enthusiasm. However, they decided to cut their losses in favour of Henry Royce's car.

The first Rolls-Royces

One outcome of the Manchester meeting was that an agreement was drawn up stipulating that C.S. Rolls and Co. would sell all the cars Royce Ltd could produce. And the resultant cars would bear the name Rolls-Royce. This may sound a trifle unfair on Royce who had, after all, designed the car but the primary use of Rolls's name made marketing and alliterative sense. This agreement was finally signed on 23 December 1904.

A more immediate outcome of the meeting, however, was that work started at once on a batch of nineteen 10 hp cars and a new model, a three-cylinder 15 hp car, was initiated. Unlike the three 10 hp prototypes, these vehicles witnessed the introduction of the famous Classically inspired radiator fitted to all Rolls-Royces thereafter. Later in 1904 meetings were held between Johnson and the Royce company when it was decided to extend the range to include four-cylinder 20 hp and six-cylinder 30 hp cars. The earlier 10 hp and these later two models, in the interests of rationalization, shared the same cylinder

blocks, pistons and connecting rods. In December 1904 C.S. Rolls and Co.'s stand at the Paris salon displayed two-, three- and four-cylinder Rolls-Royces, along with the first 30 hp six-cylinder engine. Henry Royce's cars had made their international début.

The following year Rolls moved his London showrooms from Brook Street to nearby Conduit Street, premises the company occupies to this day. He was also competitively active, which gave the new marque some valuable publicity. It so happened that Arthur Harry Briggs, a wealthy Bradford mill owner, had bought the first 20 hp car. As the 20 was the first Rolls-Royce to be capable of taking the heavy and elaborate coachwork favoured by the rich, it was designated the Heavy 20. Briggs suggested to Rolls that he should enter a lightened version of the model for the Tourist Trophy race, due to be held in the Isle of Man in September 1905. Rolls agreed with alacrity and two 20 hp chassis were prepared for the event, while Royce produced an overdrive fourth 'sprinting' gear in place of the original three-speed unit. As for the race itself, Rolls dropped out on the first lap with gearbox trouble but Percy Northey, in the second 20, went on to take second place. Consequently the Light 20 was introduced, perpetuating the TT modification, the resulting shorter and narrower chassis being 76 kg (168 lb) lighter than the Heavy 20 which continued in production.

The year 1905 also witnessed the appearance of a new Invisible Engine model, which seems to have been Claude Johnson's inspiration. The idea was that the car should resemble an electric brougham by its apparent absence of engine. So Royce adopted a more horizontally compact 3½-litre V8, which was tucked under the vehicle's floorboards. It seems that Sir Alfred Harmsworth (later Lord Northcliffe), founder of the *Daily Mail,* was also party to the model's conception because he came up with the idea of the 'Legalimit' variant. Although this looked more like a conventional car it would not exceed 32 km/h (20 mph), the legal speed limit of the day. But neither model was a success and, in all, only three V8-engined cars were built.

It soon became clear that the affairs of C.S. Rolls and Co. of London and the Manchester-based Royce Ltd required some tidying up. The obvious course of action was amalgamation and Rolls-Royce Ltd, echoing the name of the cars, was registered on 15 March 1906. This did not take account of Royce's crane-building and electrical activities

and these continued as a separate entity, surviving until Royce's death in 1933. It is an interesting aside that the assets were purchased by H.G. Morris of Loughborough who continued to make Royce cranes for some years afterwards.

But back to the affairs of 1906. Ernest Claremont became chairman of the new company with Rolls as technical managing director. Royce was chief engineer and works director and Claude Johnson commercial managing director. Royce and Johnson soon got down to the urgent business of planning a new factory as the cramped Cooke Street premises were obviously unsuitable for expansion. To finance this exercise it was subsequently decided to increase the company's £60,000 capital to £200,000 of which £100,000 would be open to public flotation.

Some timely publicity was being gained by the company in the meantime. In May 1906 Rolls, at the wheel of a Light 20, beat a record set up by Charles Jarrott the previous year when he drove a Crossley from Monte Carlo to London in 37 hours 30 minutes. Despite the fact that Rolls had to wait three hours for a boat to take him across the English Channel, he bettered Jarrott's time by one and a half minutes. Then, the following month, Claude Johnson, driving a 30 hp car, put up a faultless performance in the Scottish Reliability Trials. But the greatest victory of the year came in the 1906 Tourist Trophy race. Two Light 20s were entered and, although on this occasion Northey dropped out on the first lap (with a broken front spring), Rolls went on to win at an average speed of 63.24 km/h (39.30 mph). Not content with British successes, he took Northey's car across the Atlantic and won the Five Miles Silver Trophy for 25 hp cars at the Empire City Track, Yonkers, New York.

That year's London Motor Show was of enormous significance for Rolls-Royce. For not only did C.S. Rolls and Co.'s stand display the coveted Tourist Trophy, along with the winning car, but also a new 40/50 hp model was unveiled. A gleaming chassis was displayed and the lower half of the engine's crankcase was removed and a mirror revealed the six-cylinder power unit's internals. The model was Royce's masterpiece and was to mark a turning point in the company's affairs.

It is what we now know as the Silver Ghost, Rolls-Royce's most illustrious car.

THE
SILVER
GHOST

The creation of the Silver Ghost, as the model was retrospectively titled after its demise, reflected both Claude Johnson's desire for a longer chassis to carry larger and more elaborate coachwork and Henry Royce's wish to remedy the crankshaft failures that occurred on some of the 30 hp six-cylinder cars. Let us examine the question of chassis length first.

Rolls and Johnson, from the very outset, had looked for wealthy and aristocratic customers for Royce's products. Such sections of the community invariably chose large cars with ample carrying capacity for their immediate retinue and luggage for wintering, for instance, in Cannes or Monte Carlo. Until the appearance of the 40/50 hp Rolls-Royce, they may have bought a Mercedes or Panhard and, when British manufacturers started catering for their needs, Napier or Daimler limousines.

Now the largest capacity model that Rolls-Royce produced up until 1906 was the six-litre 30 hp car, the longest example having an overall length of 4032 mm (13 ft 2¾ in). Therefore if the company was to reap the benefits of an opulent clientele it was going to have to produce a larger car. This requirement was underlined to Johnson during 1905 by Montague Graham-White, a perceptive pioneer motorist who had designed coachwork for some of the larger French cars. Graham-White urged Rolls-Royce to produce longer chassis cars. In December 1905 he entered into an exclusive agreement with C.S. Rolls and Co. for Rolls-Royce coachwork, producing plans for limousine, Pullman, town coupé, sports four-seater tourer and speed model two-seaters. His fee was £75 per design.

The unveiling of the 40/50

The first result of this agreement appeared at the 1906 Motor Show which, as we have seen, was the occasion of the début of the 40/50. Sharing the stand with that magnificent polished chassis was a majestic Pullman limousine, built by Barker to Graham-White's design and made possible by the new 40/50 chassis. This measured 4756 mm (15 ft 7¼ in) in length, making it more than 610 mm (2 ft) longer than the largest 30 hp car.

But a larger chassis required a bigger capacity engine and it was here that Royce drew on the experience he had gained from his earlier designs, developing and refining the concept of the 30 hp six-cylinder model, which had suffered in its early days from catastrophic crankshaft failure. For early in 1906, three 30s had broken their cranks while on test and Royce immediately set about remedying the problem. It is a peculiarity of the six-cylinder engine layout that it sets up excessive torsional vibrations that, if left unchecked, will produce exactly those symptoms that Royce experienced with the 30. He succeeded in preventing these breakages by removing the crankshaft balance weights and lessening the mass of the forward flywheel.

With the 40/50, however, Royce did not initially employ a vibration damper, though an externally mounted one appeared in 1910 and this was contained within the crankcase the following year. Also by increasing the bore by half an inch and making a similar reduction in stroke, Royce assumed that he would be able to eliminate the crucial crankshaft vibration he had experienced with the 30. The crankshaft itself was considerably strengthened for the same reason. Like that on the 30, it had seven main bearings and was carried in the upper half of the aluminium crankcase, which was a great improvement on the earlier design. Another plus was the use of a fully pressurized lubrication system. The cast-iron, fixed-head cylinder blocks were arranged in two units of three pots, rather than three batches of two as with the earlier six. Also the overhead inlet valves were dispensed with, no doubt in the interests of quiet running: the 40/50's valves were all side mounted. The capacity was 7036 cc, increased to 7428 cc in 1910. As with the later 20 and 30 hp models, Royce took pains to anticipate ignition failure, a great bugbear in those days, by giving the new model a dual system, each retaining its own set of sparking plugs. One employed trembler coil accumulators coupled to coil and commutator while the other was by magneto, driven via gears off the crankshaft. The forward engine mounting was also ingenious, allowing the chassis to flex without straining the engine and also contributing to quiet running. A separately mounted four-speed gearbox was fitted, with an overdrive top, as pioneered on the Light 20, though in 1910 it was replaced by a three-speed unit.

This description can do little justice to the impact the 40/50 made on its announcement. The car's extraordinary silence, its smooth running and undoubted refinement, to which should be coupled its sheer

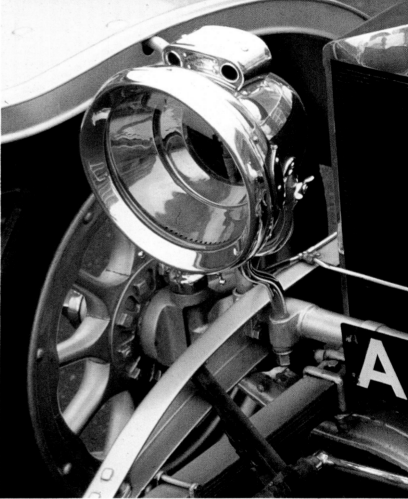

40/50 hp (Silver Ghost) (1906-25)			
ENGINE		**Wheelbase mm**	3441 (short), 3644 (long); (1923) 3657, 3822
Type	2 cast-iron fixed-head monoblocs	**Track mm**	1422
No. of cylinders	6	**Suspension – front**	Half elliptic
Bore/stroke mm	114.3 × 114.3; (1910) 114.3 × 120.6	**Suspension – rear**	Platform; (1912) cantilevers
Displacement cc	7036 (7428)	**Brakes**	Rear only. (1924) front wheel brakes and mechanical servo
Valve operation	Side		
Sparkplugs per cyl.	2		
Carburation	Royce 2-jet type	**Tyre size – front**	875 × 105 (short), 880 × 120 (long)
BHP	48 at 1200 rpm	**Tyre size – rear**	880 × 120 (short), 895 × 135 (long); (1923) 33 × 5 (front and rear)
DRIVE TRAIN			
Clutch	Cone		
Transmission	Separate 4-speed gearbox; (1910) 3-speed gearbox; (1911) torque tube	**Wheels**	Artillery with wooden spokes available to 1921; (1913) wire introduced
CHASSIS			
Frame	Channel section with gearbox subframe	**PERFORMANCE**	
		Maximum speed	111 km/h (69 mph)
		Number built	6173

PRECEDING PAGES AND ABOVE *The most famous Rolls-Royce of all: the 1907 Silver Ghost, with Roi des Belges Barker coachwork, which subsequently gave its name to the 40/50 model, and in the company's ownership since 1948. Provided by Rolls-Royce Motors Limited.*

beauty, all contributed to a magnificent car that was head and shoulders above its contemporaries. Even more significant was the decision to discontinue all other Rolls-Royces, leaving the 40/50 in splendid isolation. For if the new model was a masterpiece of design then the one-model policy was a triumph of marketing. It should be remembered that at the time most manufacturers offered a bewildering variety of models intended to capture as many tastes and pockets as possible. The credit should go to Claude Johnson for the one-model decision, which was taken in March 1908, 15 months after the 40/50's appearance. However, it should be seen against the background of a year that began with the local manager of the London City and Midland Bank having to grant Rolls-Royce a £20,000 overdraft. Johnson argued

that the development of a new four-cylinder model (in succession to the 20) would cost thousands of pounds. There was no falling off in demand for the 40/50 and there were sound reasons for a one-model policy with a saving on tooling costs in the new factory by then well under construction.

It should be remembered that the establishment of a new works had been the main reason for Rolls-Royce 'going public' in November 1906, and members of the board decided that a minimum subscription of 50,000 shares would have to be taken up before they could proceed. Unfortunately the issue did not match expectations but salvation came in the shape of the sturdy figure of Arthur Briggs, the Bradford woollen merchant who had been instrumental in convincing Rolls of the wisdom of entering the 1905 TT. By this time Briggs was a Rolls-Royce director and company secretary John de Looze had the idea of approaching him to bridge the gap. Briggs rose to the occasion and offered £10,000 on the spot. This brought the total subscription to £62,000 and plans for expansion now came closer to reality.

The original intention seems to have been to establish the new factory in Manchester. Then a further four sites were contemplated, mostly in the Midlands, and Bradford was also considered, on land owned by Arthur Briggs. But when Derby Town Council heard that Rolls-Royce was looking for a new factory site the company was offered the considerable inducement of cheap electricity on a long-term contract and the provision of all other essential services. A site was purchased from the Osmaston Estates Company and work began, Royce having the responsibility of planning the new factory and negotiating with contractors.

'The Silver Ghost'

In the meantime Claude Johnson was engaged in obtaining valuable publicity for the 40/50. He took the 13th chassis (possibly the one that had graced the 1906 show stand), had it painted with aluminium paint to give a silver finish while the Barker Roi des Belges touring body was similarly resplendent. All the appropriate metal work was then

BELOW *A 1924 Silver Ghost with limousine body by Joseph Cockshoot of Manchester, photographed at Tissington, Derby. This is one of the last series Ghosts and is fitted with front-wheel brakes, having been returned to the factory for the purpose. Provided by Rex Sevier.*

silver-plated and, as was his way, Johnson decreed that the car should be named. It was called 'The Silver Ghost', 'Silver' because of its finish and 'Ghost' to reflect its remarkable silence.

Johnson then embarked on a positive orgy of runs and reliability trials. These began in May 1907 and, as a start, Johnson took on a White steam car in a public test. He then turned north to Hatfield and headed for Scotland, travelling to Glasgow via Darlington, remaining in top gear throughout. Once north of the border, he indulged in some impressive hill climbing over the course of the forthcoming Scottish Reliability Trials. Then it was a return to Glasgow, Edinburgh and the long haul back to London and on to Bexhill in Sussex, whence he had started. This epic lasted 12 days, was under RAC scrutiny, and a fuel consumption of 13.54 litres/100 km (20.86 mpg) was achieved on the London–Glasgow stretch.

It was a remarkable performance for a 7-litre car weighing close on 2030 kg (2 tons) when complete with four occupants and equipment.

LEFT *Claude Johnson (1864-1926), Rolls-Royce's managing director, who died at the age of 61. He had worked untiringly for the company and played a crucial role in its survival.*

ABOVE *One of the last Silver Ghosts built before World War 1. This model, with touring body by Flewitt, has been owned by the same family since 1918. Chassis number is 15ED. Provided by D.K. and R.A. Lankester.*

RIGHT *The actual car driven by E.W. (later Lord) Hives from London to Edinburgh in top gear in 1911. The original body was by Brown's of Derby; the present one is the work of the car's owner. Provided by Kenneth Neve.*

A few minor adjustments had been necessary to the coil, carburettor, brakes and electrics but these had only absorbed 1 hour 28 minutes of the 12 days. This was just the start! On this occasion 3219 km (2000½ miles) had been covered but the record for non-stop running then stood at 11,408 km (7089 miles). So the Ghost was entered for the Scottish Trials, the journey north was made again and the Rolls-Royce gained a gold medal. After the Trials, the car threaded its way towards London via Glasgow, Edinburgh, Durham, Leeds, Bradford, Huddersfield, Manchester, and Coventry. Not surprisingly, the record was easily broken, being increased to more than double the existing figure to 23,128 km (14,371 miles) with involuntary stops. Afterwards the 40/50 was stripped down by RAC engineers and no measurable wear was found in the engine, transmission, brakes or steering gear. A minute amount of play was discovered in the rear spring shackles, pivot pins and magneto drive, but The Silver Ghost was in 'all respects... good running order' concluded the RAC. With these records under his belt, Johnson loaded his family aboard that remarkable 40/50 and took them off for a Cornish holiday.

Work was progressing apace on the new Rolls-Royce factory at Nightingale Road, Derby, and it was duly opened on 8 July 1908 by Lord Montagu of Beaulieu, a friend of Rolls and Johnson, and champion of motorists' rights in the House of Lords. Derby was destined to be the home of Rolls-Royce cars until the outbreak of World War 2 in 1939.

The Rolls-Royce board members clearly felt that Johnson's remarkable 1907 feats with The Silver Ghost had served the company's purpose for, in July 1908, he got their approval that no more cars should be entered by the firm for trials, records or similar events. Although they undoubtedly gained the 40/50 valuable publicity, such feats were extremely expensive to stage.

Royce's ill health and its consequences

Claude Johnson's role in Rolls-Royce affairs was becoming increasingly important and, in March 1909, he was promoted from commercial managing director to chief executive. During the year, fears continued to grow about Royce's health, and in January 1910 it was announced that he had curtailed all his executive duties to concentrate fully on technical matters, taking the title of engineer-in-chief. It was the start

of a difficult year for the young company and the fact that it emerged relatively unscathed says much for Johnson's steadying hand.

After the attempt to ease Royce's work load came Charles Rolls's request to the board to relieve him of his 'irksome' duties. Then, in April, he resigned as a director of the company that bore his name. In truth, he had become totally absorbed in the world of aviation which initially had taken a tandem role with his motoring interests. A few months after he had left Rolls-Royce, on 12 July, he was tragically killed in a flying accident at Bournemouth. He was 32 years old. (His father, Lord Llangattock, died two years later and the title was inherited by the eldest brother John who was killed in 1916 during World War 1. The second brother, Henry, died just before John and with no further sons the Llangattock title became extinct.)

Royce, deeply affected by the death of Rolls, suffered a collapse in his own health. A complete rest was prescribed and Henry went to recuperate at the Norfolk seaside village of Overstrand, just south of Cromer. As it had become essential for him to receive professional nursing, Miss Ethel Aubin was provided by a local nursing home. She was destined to remain with Henry Royce until his death in 1933 and the fact that he survived until the age of 70, indeed outliving Claude Johnson, says much for Ethel Aubin's diligence and devotion.

It was decided that the South of France would provide the best possible climate for Royce's convalescence, so he and Nurse Aubin crossed the Channel and travelled to Tours by train. There they met up with Claude Johnson and a 40/50 fitted with a magnificent Barker double enclosed Pullman limousine body and named 'The Charmer'. They motored south to the village of Le Canadel on the French Riviera where

Johnson already owned a house called Villa Jaune. Royce was captivated by the place, so Johnson immediately put arrangements in hand for the purchase of land adjoining his own grounds. Royce himself designed his house, which initially was called Les Cypres, changed in 1914 to Villa Mimosa. Soon after his first visit in 1911 Royce was taken seriously ill. A 40/50, converted to take an ambulance body, was swiftly dispatched to Le Canadel and he was driven back across France and on to London where major surgery was carried out by his doctor and old friend Campbell-Thompson. Fortunately Royce recovered from the operation and went to live for a time in Crowborough, Sussex; although he was visited by his wife Minnie, their marriage was at an end and thereafter he was solely dependent on Ethel Aubin.

Royce's illness, although it caused Johnson an enormous amount of time and effort, was to prove something of a blessing in disguise, both for the engineer-in-chief and the Rolls-Royce company. For in truth Royce was something of a liability at Derby: such is often the way with genius. His endless quest for mechanical perfection meant that there were constant interruptions with the process of production. He would not tolerate the slightest sloppiness among his workforce and was quite capable of dismissing an employee for the most trivial shortcoming. Clearly this could not go on and Royce's illness and resultant indisposition produced an elaborate compromise that, although somewhat unwieldy in concept, worked fairly well until his death in 1933. He was to spend the summer months, along with his design team, on the south coast of England, first at St Margaret's Bay, Kent, near Johnson's own house, and later, in 1917, at West Wittering, Sussex. Winter time was spent on the French Riviera at his beloved Le Canadel, with his staff who worked in a special building known as La Bureau. So it was that after leaving the Derby factory in 1910, Royce, except for one occasion, never returned.

Amazingly Johnson found time in 1911 to initiate yet another useful publicity exercise. Prior to the appearance of the 40/50 Rolls-Royce, Napier could justly claim to be Britain's leading make and exponent of the six-cylinder car. But the roles were reversed, as it were, for the new Rolls-Royce quickly eroded the prestige of the Napier and soon surpassed it, which must have caused the Acton company some

consternation—and its publicist extraordinary, Selwyn Francis Edge. He therefore took a 65 hp Napier, mildly tuned it, and proceeded to drive from London to Edinburgh in top gear, smartly following up with a run around Brooklands race track. The results of this RAC-observed exercise made impressive reading. The Napier had achieved an average fuel consumption of 14.6 litres/100 km (19.35 mpg) and attained a maximum speed of 123 km/h (76.42 mph).

The 40/50 in the trials again
Although Rolls-Royce had vowed to avoid such contests, Johnson felt that the Napier gauntlet could not go unchallenged and a slightly modified 40/50 was prepared for the purpose. Departures from standard included underslung rear suspension, increased compression ratio and improved carburation, and the bodywork was rather rakish, with a tapered bonnet and lightweight wings. Although the 40/50 was of slightly smaller capacity, it beat the Napier on both counts, returning an overall fuel consumption, from London to Edinburgh, of 11.6 litres/100 km/h (24.32 mpg) while afterwards the car clocked a respectable top speed of 126 km/h (78.26 mph). It was an inspired decision on the company's part to market this variant, with the aforementioned modifications, as the London-Edinburgh model, regarded by many as the finest 40/50 of all.

By this time the original four-speed overdrive gearbox had been replaced by a three-speed unit. It was a modification that the company was to regret the following year when James Radley, driving a London-Edinburgh model, having entered the 1912 Alpine Trial, found that he was only able to climb the 1 in 4 Katschberg Pass by unloading two of his passengers. As this was about as unlikely an event as the German Kaiser breaking into a spirited rendering of *Rule Britannia*, Rolls-Royce responded by preparing a team of three cars for the following year's event. The cars used for the 1913 Alpine Trial were a synthesis of the London-Edinburgh specifications and a Colonial model 40/50 with a higher ground clearance, larger capacity radiator and a four-speed gearbox which, unlike that on the original 40/50, had a direct-drive fourth gear. The four Rolls-Royces (Radley again competed) dominated the Trial and only missed the team prize by a

whisker when one of the cars was in collision with a non-competing Minerva. Corporate and national prestige was restored, underlined in 1914 when Radley again entered and was the only competitor in his class not to lose marks. While chronicling the 40/50's competition successes, it is perhaps surprising to find that in 1913 one took first place in that year's Spanish Grand Prix with the company's agent, Carlos de Salamanca, at the wheel. Another example, driven by Eric Platford, was third.

Mention should be made of the famous Spirit of Ecstasy mascot, commissioned by Johnson, who felt that the motifs that some customers used to grace their Rolls-Royces were hardly worthy of the

welded-on water jackets: early on those leaking welds became bywords among pilots and navigators, and chewing gum consumption by air crew rose accordingly. The Eagle was followed by the six-cylinder Hawk, the 12-cylinder Falcon and, after the war, the Condor. The last-named was, in effect, a scaled-up version of the Eagle but with four valves per cylinder instead of two.

With this momentum established, Rolls-Royce moved decisively into the aero engine field. It was a market that was to be consolidated in the 1920s and expanded in the '30s to such an extent that by mid-decade Rolls-Royce was principally an aero engine manufacturer. In fact, the cars relied on profits generated in this lucrative market.

PRECEDING PAGES *1914 Silver Ghost. The chassis was shipped to Australia in July 1914 and the touring body is by Waring Brothers of Melbourne. It was exported to America in May 1972. Provided by Dick Philippi.*

LEFT *A Silver Ghost-based armoured car on active service during World War 1. Armament was a Vickers .303 machine gun, and a crew of four was carried.*

RIGHT *A 1913 Silver Ghost town carriage by Mulliner. Provided by Merle Norman Classic Beauty Collection.*

make. He therefore commissioned artist Charles Sykes to produce a company-approved mascot which was originally titled 'The Spirit of Speed'. Johnson was familiar with Sykes's work for he had already executed a series of paintings for the company that were later used in its lavish sales catalogues. It is possible that Sykes had been introduced to Johnson by Lord Montagu of Beaulieu. Tradition insists that the model for the superb Art Nouveau mascot was Eleanor Thornton, his lordship's secretary, in whom Sykes took more than a passing interest. Although Sykes conveyed the resulting statuette to Rolls-Royce in 1911 the mascot produced from it did not enjoy popular currency until after World World 1. Royce himself would never fit one. He considered that it spoiled the bonnet line.

Royce starts designing aero engines

The outbreak of World War 1 in 1914 was to have an enormous and far-reaching effect on the Rolls-Royce company. This was because Britain was suffering from an almost total absence of home-produced aero engines. It is sobering to recall that, when war broke out, the Royal Flying Corps and the Royal Naval Air Service had not a single aircraft powered by a British aero engine. Those they did have were mostly of French manufacture, namely by Gnôme, Renault or Le Rhône. This was an unsatisfactory situation in time of peace, but potentially disastrous in war. As Rolls-Royce's Derby works was one of the country's most up-to-date car factories it was not surprising that in August 1914, the very month that war broke out, the Admiralty should ask the company to design an aero engine.

As ever, Claude Johnson's principal concern was the precarious state of Royce's health but, as he had refused to go to Le Canadel when war broke out, he settled down at St Margaret's Bay with A. G. Elliott and Maurice Olley and began work on the design of a water-cooled V12 engine: the prototype Eagle. However, before this power unit became a reality, Rolls-Royce manufactured some Renault and Royal Aircraft Factory 1A engines and, although this output continued into 1916, by that time the Eagle was well into production. Deliveries began in October 1915 and continued right through the war years and beyond, ceasing in 1924. This engine, the first of a distinguished line, has a fascinating parentage for it had been inspired, in part, by the power unit of a Mercedes racing car of the type that won the celebrated French Grand Prix of 1914. As it happened, one of the victorious trio was in England when war broke out, so its engine was removed and sent to Derby. There Royce went to examine it—the only occasion he returned to the Nightingale Road works after his 1910 illness. The Eagle reveals its Mercedes influence by Royce's use of separate

The Rolls-Royce armoured car

No reference to Rolls-Royce and World War 1 would be complete without mention of the 40/50-based armoured car. Although rather basic conversions were available as early as September 1914, later these Rolls-Royces saw service in practically every theatre of war, from the Western Front to German West Africa. But although conditions hardly lent themselves to their extensive use in France and there were not sufficient machines to make a tremendous impact, nevertheless in the sands of North Africa and Arabia these armoured cars really proved their worth.

A particularly daring rescue occurred in 1915 when the crew of the torpedoed British ship *Tara* was held in the Sahara desert by Senussi tribesmen operating on the Turks' behalf. Under the command of the Duke of Westminster, 45 vehicles, most of them Rolls-Royce armoured cars, travelling by night and day, covered 193 km (120 miles) in 14 hours to rescue the crew in truly dramatic style. T. E. Lawrence has also immortalized Rolls-Royce armoured cars and tenders in his inspired chronicle of his Arabian adventures, *The Seven Pillars of Wisdom.* Incredibly these armoured cars employed the basic 40/50 chassis, although twin rear wheels were fitted to cope with the increased weight of the armour-plated bodywork. The protective radiator doors, which could be closed when the vehicle was in action, did contribute to boiling but, this shortcoming apart, these Rolls-Royces enhanced the company's magnificent reliability record. Thus prestige was sharpened by conflict.

Before leaving the subject of these extraordinary vehicles, it should be noted that after the war they were progressively modified to become the longest-serving British armoured car. The 1924 Pattern even saw service in World War 2 and took part in Libyan operations in 1941-2.

With the signing of the Armistice in November 1918, Rolls-Royce turned again to the production of the 40/50 for civilian use. Then, in June 1919, the company's already enhanced reputation received a further boost when the British aviators John William Alcock and Arthur Whitten Brown made the first non-stop trans-Atlantic flight in a Vickers Vimy, powered by a pair of Rolls-Royce Eagle engines. The same year the 40/50 was re-introduced with a few improvements to the 1914 specifications. In came aluminium pistons, which had been fitted to the London-Edinburgh and Alpine models just before the war. This was an improvement that the car's owner would have been unaware of, but the introduction of a chain-driven electric starter was a far more obvious refinement. Royce had decreed in 1917 that the post-war cars should be improved in this way. He was no doubt aware that the American Cadillac had offered the device as a standard fitment since 1914.

A HOST OF PHANTOMS

The two years that followed the end of World War 1 witnessed an unprecedented boom in Britain. The pent-up frustrations of war resulted in a financial and emotional uplift that withered away at the end of 1920. The following year was dominated by a terrible depression, high unemployment and the collapse of many companies created in those heady post-war months. Claude Johnson was only too aware of these changes, and that the 40/50 was a child of the Edwardian era: those sunny days when, for the Rolls-Royce clientele, it was always afternoon. The harsher realities of the 1920s convinced Johnson that Rolls-Royce must produce a smaller car more suited to the times. The outcome was the 20 hp car of 1922 and it marked the beginning of a two-model policy that continues to this very day. This smaller car, and its inter-war derivatives, are considered later (see pages 52-61).

The New Phantom

Meanwhile the Rolls-Royce board was contemplating the future of the 40/50. In truth, it was beginning to look its age and was becoming increasingly expensive to manufacture. After all, Royce had conceived the car back in 1906 and since then there had been enormous progress in automobile design, which had been stimulated by the technological advances of war. So, in September 1922, it was decided that work

PRECEDING PAGES A Croyden convertible by Brewster. A Derby-built left-hand drive Phantom II of 1932. Provided by Merle Norman Classic Beauty Collection.

should begin on a 40/50 replacement though the car that emerged in May 1925 was, in effect, simply a new engine fitted in the 40/50 chassis. It was announced that the new model would be called the New Phantom and the older car would henceforth be titled the Silver Ghost, a tribute to that famous and much-publicized 1907 example.

The new engine was only slightly larger than that fitted in the Silver Ghost, 7668 cc compared with 7428 cc. Inevitably it was a six-cylinder, though the Ghost's fixed cylinder head side-valve layout was replaced by a single detachable cylinder head containing pushrod-operated overhead valves. But, like the earlier model, the cylinders were cast in two batches of three and, as with the Ghost, the Phantom was offered with dual ignition: magneto and coil, each firing its own sparking plug, there being two per cylinder. The contrast of aluminium crankcase and black stove-enamelled cylinder block provided an impressive visual impact and the new engine, with its overhead valves, sat rather higher under the New Phantom's bonnet than the old side-valve engine had

BELOW Built for diamond magnate Otto Oppenheimer, this 1928 Phantom I is known as The Black Diamond. Coachwork is by Hooper and all the interior and exterior fittings are silver plated. There is a secret compartment in the car for the safe transit of diamonds.

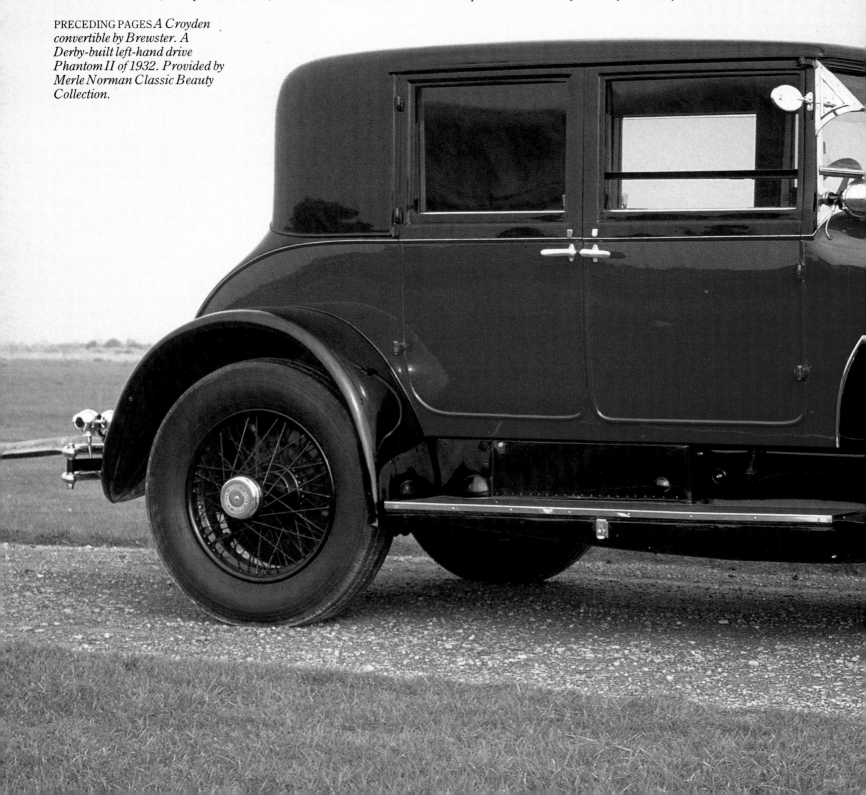

New Phantom (Phantom I)
(1925-9)

ENGINE

Type	2 cast-iron monoblocs, each of 3 cylinders, with detachable iron cylinder head, (1928) aluminium; on aluminium crankcase
No. of cylinders	6
Bore/stroke mm	107.9 × 139.7
Displacement cc	7668
Valve operation	Pushrod overhead
Sparkplugs per cyl.	2
Compression ratio	4:1
Carburation	Rolls-Royce 2-jet type
BHP	108 at 2300 rpm

DRIVE TRAIN

Clutch	Single dry plate
Transmission	Separate 4-speed gearbox

CHASSIS

Frame	Channel section with gearbox subframe
Wheelbase mm	3638 (short), 3822 (long)
Track – front mm	1447 (short), 1485 (long)
Track – rear mm	1422 (short), 1460 (long)
Suspension – front	Semi elliptic
Suspension – rear	Cantilever
Brakes	4-wheel internal expanding with mechanical servo
Tyre size	700 × 21
Wheels	Wire

PERFORMANCE

Maximum speed	125 km/h (78 mph)
Number built	2212

done in the Silver Ghost. (The New Phantom was retrospectively known as the Phantom I.)

As already recounted, the chassis was basically Ghost so, as with the older car, transmission was by torque tube and the gearbox was mounted separately from the engine, but a single dry-plate clutch replaced the 40/50's cone one. Other visual changes were few and far between. The last of the Ghosts had been fitted with thermostatic coolant control but the Phantom, like the 20, relied on manually operated radiator shutters, though they were vertically rather than horizontally mounted. Two chassis lengths were offered, costing £1850 and £1900 respectively.

How front wheel brakes were adopted

There was, however, one improvement the Phantom enjoyed that had also featured on the 1924 Silver Ghosts. This was the fitting of front wheel brakes; how Rolls-Royce came to use them is worth telling.

Although front wheel brakes had made sporadic appearances on British cars in pre-World War 1 days, after the conflict the Continentals quickly took them up. And of the many systems employed, one of the finest was that fitted to the H6 Hispano-Suiza of 1919. The car had been designed by the talented Swiss engineer Marc Birkigt and was probably the greatest rival to the 40/50's supremacy. But it should be said that the Rolls-Royce was already 13 years old when the H6 made its début at the 1919 Paris salon. Birkigt had been responsible for the design of the V8 Hispano-Suiza aero engine, the most widely used Allied power unit of the war. For his car, he had taken the concept of a later V12 version and, on dividing it, came up with a 6597 cc six-cylinder overhead-camshaft engine. The outcome was an engineering and aesthetic triumph.

It was not long before Royce had a Hispano-Suiza for scrutiny at Elmstead, his West Wittering home and design office, where he had moved in 1917. The year was 1921 and, taking the H6's braking system as his starting point, he proceeded to improve and refine the concept until it satisfied his own high standards. In November 1923 it was announced that front wheel brakes would be fitted to the 1924 40/50s. The system was both ingenious and efficient. It relied on a power take-off from the gearbox which was transferred to the braking system via friction discs. When the brake pedal was applied this servo assistance operated the front brakes and also contributed to actuating the rear ones. From 1924 this arrangement became an integral part of the Rolls-Royce car right up until 1966 when the Silver Cloud III ceased production, and even until 1978 on the majestic Phantom VI.

It was therefore a natural progression for the New Phantom to benefit from these brakes. Although this car remained in production until 1929, it cannot be regarded as the company's most inspired model. A change in mechanical specifications came in 1928 with the adoption of an aluminium cylinder head but, in truth, that high Edwardian chassis looked a little awkward in the 1920s for, after all, only the engine had been designed in the post-war years.

Then tragedy overtook Rolls-Royce management. In April 1926 Claude Johnson caught a chill that quickly turned to pneumonia and he died at his London home at Adelphi Terrace on 11 April at the age of 61. Royce, on hearing the news, remarked: 'He was the captain. We were only the crew.' How right he was. Johnson's genius had honed and refined the Rolls-Royce image so that it became the most venerated marque name in the world. He had worked untiringly for the company, though much of his energy was absorbed in his later years in Rolls-Royce's unprofitable American venture at Springfield, Massachusetts, which is detailed later (see pages 42-51). He was succeeded as managing director by his brother Basil, but this proved a short-lived appointment and in 1929 he was replaced by Arthur Sidgreaves. Educated at the well-known Downside School, Sidgreaves had worked for Napier before joining Rolls-Royce in 1920, and at the time of his appointment he was the company's general sales manager.

ABOVE *Far from home and away from the city lights, this 1926 Phantom I town car by Binder is now in America. The sedanca de ville coachwork took little account of the chauffeur's comfort. Provided by Lester J. Harris.*

LEFT *Another sedanca de ville but this time by Hooper. The car is a 1927 Phantom I and has the distinction of having been in the same family since new. Provided by Mrs Alan Kilpatrick.*

ABOVE RIGHT *The most illustrious Rolls-Royce of the inter-war years: the Continental Phantom II. This 1933 short-chassis example is an Owner Driver Saloon by Park Ward. What better way to travel to Cannes or Monte Carlo in the 1930s? The car's chassis number is 72MY. Provided by Tom Mason.*

Phantom II (1929-35)			
ENGINE		**CHASSIS**	
Type	2 cast-iron monoblocs, each of 3 cylinders, with detachable aluminium cylinder head, on aluminium crankcase	Frame	Channel section
		Wheelbase mm	3657 (short), 3810 (long)
		Track mm	1485
		Suspension – front	Half elliptic
No. of cylinders	6	Suspension – rear	Half elliptic
Bore/stroke mm	107.9 × 139.7	Brakes	4-wheel internal expanding with mechanical servo
Displacement cc	7668		
Valve operation	Pushrod overhead	Tyre size	700 × 21; (1930) 700 × 20; (1933) 700 × 19
Sparkplugs per cyl.	2		
Compression ratio	4.75:1		
Carburation	Rolls-Royce 2-jet type	Wheels	Wire
BHP	120 at 3000 rpm	**PERFORMANCE (Continental)**	
		Maximum speed	148 km/h (92.3 mph)
DRIVE TRAIN			
Clutch	Single dry plate	Acceleration	0-60 mph 19.6 sec
Transmission	Integral 4-speed gearbox	Number built	1767

The Phantom II

In 1929, the year that Sidgreaves took up his appointment, Rolls-Royce announced the successor to the New Phantom, the Phantom II. Although the engine was substantially the same, the gearbox was now in unit with it but, above all, the new car had a simpler and lower chassis frame, similar in concept to the smaller 20 hp model. It was therefore fitted with half elliptic springs all round, whereas the Phantom I had retained cantilevers at the rear, which betrayed its Edwardian origins. The new car in closed form had its overall height reduced by 230 mm (9 in) compared with its lofty Phantom I equivalent. But, most important of all as far as the Rolls-Royce story is concerned, it was the last design that Royce saw through from beginning to end.

A highly skilled and distinguished team was responsible for the design of Rolls-Royce cars at this time, which, of course, means the Phantom II. Royce himself was no draughtsman. He used to jot his ideas down on scraps of paper, or on the backs of envelopes, and they would then be handed on to a designer to interpret. Once the drawings were produced, Royce could read them with great rapidity and project the function and working of the component in his mind's eye. Royce's senior engine designer was Albert Elliott, who had joined Rolls-Royce from Napier in 1912 and headed the design team from 1917 until 1932. Gearbox, propeller shaft and rear axle design came within the orbit of W.G. 'Bill' Hardy, who had worked for Clement-Talbot before joining the company in 1921. Chassis, suspension, steering axles and brakes were the responsibility of Bernard Day, formerly of Sheffield-Simplex. Ivan Evernden looked after body design and mountings and, as we shall

see, was to play an important role in the creation of the Phantom II and its magnificent derivative, the fabled Continental model.

Drawings for the new model were produced by Royce's team by March 1928 and the prototype chassis was running by the end of the year. The bodywork was a supremely elegant Barker sports saloon designed by Evernden. Royce had been much impressed by the Riley Nine Monaco saloon and was particularly attracted by the fact that the passengers sat within the wheelbase, instead of the more usual arrangement in which the rear occupants were directly over the rear axle. Not that the Riley influence stopped there!

After the Phantom II had gone into production, Royce conceived the idea of producing a 'tuned-up' version, a project in which the company's sales staff showed little interest. However, he decided to pursue the idea on his own account with Evernden's assistance, and his starting point was the aforementioned Phantom II prototype. He took the shorter 3.66 m (12 ft) chassis that was offered on the model's announcement. To this was fitted a tuned engine and a high-ratio rear axle and specially raked steering column. Evernden was then dispatched to the Riley agents in Guildford to purchase a Riley Nine saloon. The Riley was then dismantled, for Royce wanted to study the way that the close-coupled effect had been achieved. The four seats on the Nine were contained within the wheelbase by making the rear floor lower than the front, which allowed the back passengers' feet access to wells below the front seats. Fortunately, with this experimental Phantom it was not necessary to go to the same lengths as the Riley. Evernden therefore designed a four-door saloon and incorporated the

33

then relatively new Hooper 'sunshine roof'. The front wings were particularly striking. They were stylishly flared and perfectly complemented the car's sporting ambience.

The construction of the body was entrusted to Barker and Royce dictated that the car should be finished in a light colour. So the body and wings were painted in a delicate shade of saxe blue. It was then coated with an artificial pearl lacquer, produced by finely grinding herring scales. The effect must have been sensational, with the light-blue bodywork gleaming through a shimmering 'oyster shell' finish. Similarly the interior was a model of delicacy. The soft calf hide had been specially imported from France and echoed the colour of the bodywork; the headlining was of a slightly lighter hue. The interior wood was sycamore and also faintly azure tinted. The car was completed in August 1930, just four months after it had been conceived. It was taken down to West Wittering and Evernden later remembered that Royce first saw the car on a beautiful day with 'blue sky, blue sea and pearl blue car to match'.

Thus the Continental Phantom II model was born and it was with this car that Royce returned to the concept of his London-to-Edinburgh Silver Ghost. Had Claude Johnson lived he would surely have approved of this supreme creation.

Bentley Motors purchased

One of the cars that represented a British challenge to the Phantom II was the 6½-litre Bentley and its later 8-litre derivative. Walter Owen Bentley had founded Bentley Motors in Cricklewood, North London, in 1919. His first model had been a 3-litre sporting car with overhead-camshaft engine which eventually went into production in 1921. This was joined by a rather more sophisticated six-cylinder 6½-litre model in 1926, a car far more in the Rolls-Royce tradition. However, these developments should be seen against a background of constant under-capitalization. In 1924 the company had made a £56,700 loss and the following year it was liquidated and reorganized. Fortunately Woolf Barnato, whose father had made his millions in the South African diamond rush, was also an enthusiastic racing driver.
He put Bentley back on its feet by investing close on £143,000 in the company and under this more assured patronage a new 4½-litre

34

ABOVE *One of the advantages the Phantom II had over its predecessor was its lower chassis frame, convincingly displayed by this magnificent 1932 example. The original owner was Prince Aly Khan and the Thrupp and Maberly coachwork is unusual because it is a fixed-head coupé with a sliding roof, although the appearance suggests a drophead one. This car has remained in the same ownership for 30 years.*
Provided by Richard Lowe.

RIGHT *A magnificent head-on view of a 1933 Continental Phantom II with coachwork by Park Ward. The radiator badge was changed from red to black in this year which coincided with Sir Henry Royce's death. Note the twin spare wheels, essential equipment for touring on the Continent.*
Provided by John A. Young.

four-cylinder model appeared in 1928. Finally, for 1931 came the fabled 8-litre, a derivative of the earlier 6½-litre model. Potentially the 8-litre was the company's most profitable car, but it depended on a wealthy clientele who were attracted by the Bentley's speed and majestic appearance coupled with the marque's undoubted sporting appeal. For Bentleys had chalked up an impressive series of wins at the Le Mans 24-hour race (in 1924 and 1927-30) with, not surprisingly, Woolf Barnato sharing the winning car on the last three occasions.

In 1929 Bentley managed its only significant profit of the decade when it achieved a £28,467 surplus. But, inevitably, the Wall Street crash of that year badly damaged Bentley's precarious market and, unlike Rolls-Royce, there were no aero engine interests on which to fall back. Finances deteriorated to such an extent that in June 1931 J.K. Carruth, Bentley's managing director, attempted to salvage something from Barnato's considerable investment and wrote to Rolls-Royce's Arthur Sidgreaves, suggesting amalgamation. But the Rolls-Royce board could see little advantage in the prospect and turned the offer down. Soon afterwards, the London Life Association called in its loans and Bentley Motors was liquidated. But Napier, Rolls-Royce's arch-rivals from pre-World War 1 days, decided to purchase Bentley's assets for £103,675 and re-enter the luxury car market. The resulting vehicle would undoubtedly have presented Rolls-Royce with a formidable challenge, so Sidgreaves instructed the company's solicitors

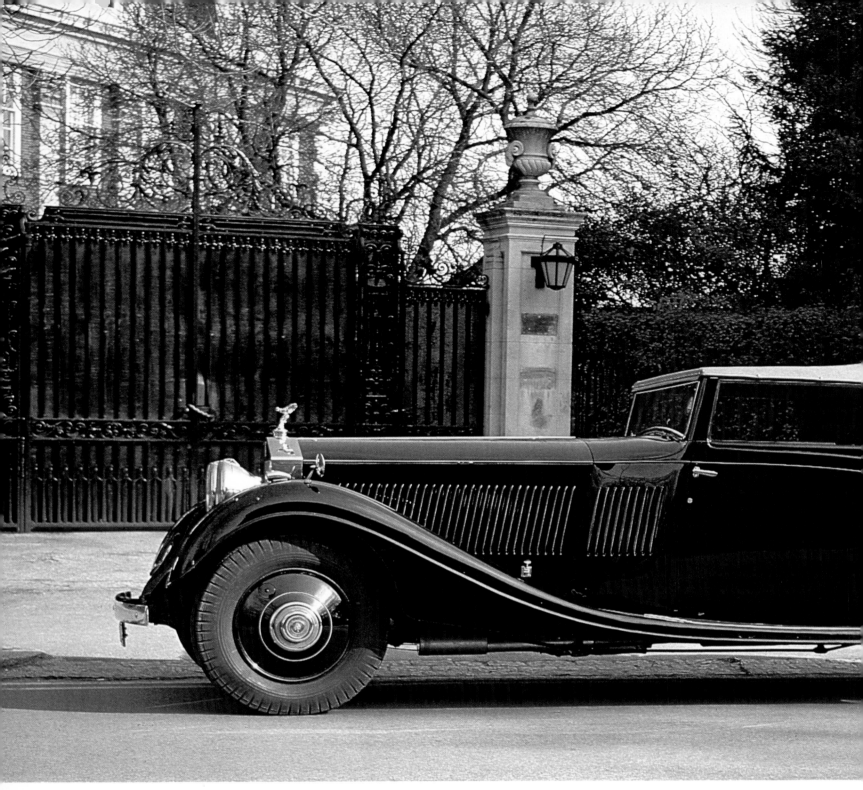

to bid for Bentley. But it was then realized that this would probably mean a rise in the asking price, so the British Equitable Trust was appointed the company's agent to bid on its behalf. This the Trust duly did and Rolls-Royce succeeded in buying the Bentley company for £125,175. W. O. Bentley remained with Napier for a short time but Sidgreaves persuaded him to join Rolls-Royce with the rather indecisive title of 'technical adviser to the managing director'. But Bentley was unable to have any design influence and when, in 1935, London lawyer Alan Good succeeded in buying the moribund Lagonda company (for which Rolls-Royce also bid), Bentley joined him as technical director. With him went Stewart Tresilian and they produced a direct challenge to the Rolls-Royce luxury market in the shape of the V12 Lagonda of 1938.

In the meantime Rolls-Royce had another string to its manufacturing bow with the ownership of the Bentley name. As far back as 1926 Henry Royce had shown some interest in designing a sports car and, after the purchase of Bentley, he set about experimenting with a supercharged engine. The intention was to use it to power a new Bentley which at this stage was based on the Peregrine, a project that might have been a cheaper version of the Rolls-Royce 20/25 (see page 57). But there were problems with the experimental engine so instead a

38

PRECEDING PAGES *Miss Betty Carstairs of London was the original owner of this stylish short-chassis 1931 Continental Phantom II with coachwork by James Young of Bromley, Kent. It is now in America. The compartment revealed behind the front seat could be used for carrying golf clubs. The chassis number is 20MS. Provided by Briggs Cunningham Automotive Museum.*

ABOVE *As it should be. This supremely elegant 1934 Continental Phantom II sedanca drophead coupé by Gurney Nutting has never needed restoration and thus retains its original paintwork. The car has been in the present owner's possession for 24 years. Provided by Jim Bidwell-Topham.*

RIGHT *The Phantom III was V12-powered and the first Rolls-Royce to employ independent front suspension. The vast majority were closed cars and this 1937 example, with Mulliner coachwork, is no exception. It was the last model in which Royce had a hand, but he never lived to see the design completed. It also has the doubtful distinction of being the last Rolls-Royce to be conceived with a seeming disregard to development costs. The car is now on display in America. Provided by Briggs Cunningham Automotive Museum.*

tuned version of the 20/25 power unit was fitted in the Peregrine chassis. This was developed into the Silent Sports Car, the 3½-litre Bentley of 1933. Therefore subsequent Bentley models benefited from the continual development of the smaller cars in the Rolls-Royce range.

The Phantom III

Of course, all these activities were taking place at a time when the world depression was at its nadir and it is a curious paradox that during these years luxury cars became increasingly more complex. In America, particularly, the V12 engine was enjoying some popularity. General Motors had the V12 Cadillac and Ford offered the Lincoln marque with a V12 engine from 1932. Packard, with a V12 tradition stretching back to 1916, was yet another American manufacturer to offer this configuration. Hispano-Suiza, Rolls-Royce's great Continental rival, had adopted the V12 in 1931. Bearing in mind that the layout was established Rolls-Royce aero engine practice, it was perhaps inevitable that the Phantom II's replacement should follow suit. The Phantom III, as the new model was called, represented the end of an era for Rolls-Royce, for it was the last model to be built regardless of cost; it required both a new engine *and* chassis; and Royce had a hand in its conception. But sophisticated as the new car was, somehow the magic of the Phantom II had been lost.

Work on the new Phantom began in the summer of 1932 and its conception marked a crisis for Royce and his design team. In December 1931 he set out from England for his annual recuperation at Le Canadel, his villa on the French Riviera, but left most of his design team at West Wittering. A. G. Elliott, who it will be recalled had worked with Royce since those dark World War 1 days, departed to Derby where he formed his own design staff. Royce returned to West Wittering in April 1932 and, on finding that Elliott had left, became deeply distressed and called his engineers and draughtsmen together and gave them the option of leaving. But they resolved to stay on, and work continued on the design of the new car, though Royce became increasingly convinced that he would never live to see the Phantom III completed. His prediction was to be proved tragically correct and much of the early months of 1933 were spent with Royce confined to his bed. He was visited in March by his old friend and doctor Campbell-Thompson, who afterwards confided in Evernden and the design team that the end was not far off.

The death of Royce

Although unable to leave his bed, Royce continued working. He designed a cottage for one of his farm workers and Evernden was dispatched to London to get the plans copied as there was no one available locally to do the job. While Evernden was in the capital, Nurse Aubin sent him a telegram to return to West Wittering immediately. As soon as he received this, Evernden caught the first available train but arrived too late. Frederick Henry Royce died at 7 am on 22 April 1933. He had lived to his 70th year.

The body was transferred from West Wittering in a Silver Ghost hearse for cremation. There was some problem in getting Royce's coffin down the narrow stairs of Elmstead. Outside the old Ghost quietly ticked over. Evernden, moved by the circumstances, regarded

this as a wonderful tribute to Henry Royce. After cremation, his ashes were taken to Number One shop at Derby and there they remained until the outbreak of World War 2. Then Ethel Aubin (who had become Mrs Tildesley) arranged for them to be removed to Alwalton parish church in the village of his birth. Thus Henry Royce's ashes were finally laid to rest.

Inevitably Royce's place at the head of the design team was taken by Elliott, and work continued apace at Derby on the Phantom III. Code-named Spectre, the new car was announced in October 1935 at a chassis price of £1850—and for the first time a Phantom was offered at a single chassis length. The 7338 cc V12 engine was a complex masterpiece, but it has to be said that Elliott paid more attention to mechanical refinement than the practicalities of a potential owner running one. The crankcase was cast in Hiduminium, an aluminium alloy developed by Rolls-Royce for its aero engine work, and produced by High Duty Alloys (hence its name). The cylinder heads were of the same material. Wet liners were employed and the overhead valves were actuated, via pushrods, from a central camshaft which, as on every Rolls-Royce engine from 1904 to the present day, was gear rather than chain driven. As if this innovation was not enough, the Phantom III was the first Rolls-Royce to be fitted with independent front suspension, and a General Motors-derived coil and wishbone layout was adopted.

Of all the Phantoms produced during the inter-war years, the III achieved the least sales (717), compared with 2212 Phantom Is and 1767 IIs. Undoubtedly the prevailing economic climate was a factor but the Phantom III did experience a variety of teething troubles, uncharacteristic of the marque, before or since. In the first instance

the V12 engine was plagued with some fairly crucial development problems. Just 12 months before the car's announcement, the company was experiencing severe slow-running difficulties and a complete cylinder head redesign was contemplated. But, by the end of 1934, this particular trouble had been narrowed down to camshaft problems. There were also carburation difficulties and, although originally four single units had been envisaged, eventually a single downdraught Stromberg was fitted, the first Phantom to employ a proprietary carburettor. This produced another set of problems because the heads had been designed for four carburettors and had six inlet ports whereas the single unit demanded four. For the first three years of production the Phantom III was fitted with its original cylinder heads, the four-port unit not arriving until 1938. As a result brake horsepower was increased from 189 to 207.

Phantom III (1935-9)			
ENGINE		**CHASSIS**	
Type	60° V Hiduminium combined crankcase and block with wet cylinder liners and Hiduminium cylinder heads	Frame	Box section with central cruciform
		Wheelbase mm	3606
		Track – front mm	1536
		Track – rear mm	1587
		Suspension – front	Independent, wishbone and coil spring
No. of cylinders	12		
Bore/stroke mm	82.5 × 114.3	Suspension – rear	Half elliptic
Displacement cc	7340	Brakes	4-wheel internal expanding with mechanical servo
Valve operation	Pushrod overhead		
Sparkplugs per cyl.	2		
Compression ratio	6:1	Tyre size	700 × 18
Carburation	Stromberg downdraught	Wheels	Wire
BHP	189 at 3650 rpm		
		PERFORMANCE	
DRIVE TRAIN		Maximum speed	140 km/h (86.96 mph)
Clutch	Single dry plate		
Transmission	Separate 4-speed gearbox	Acceleration	0-60 mph 16.8 sec
		Number built	717

LEFT AND ABOVE *A reminder that it was possible to create a really elegant Phantom III. This 1936 example was built for heiress Barbara Hutton and the body is by the French coachbuilders, Saoutchik. Provided by Briggs Cunningham Automotive Museum.*

But Phantom III owners were already suffering from a variety of under-bonnet problems, namely overheating, high oil consumption and block corrosion. If this was not enough there were fuel-pump troubles and undue camshaft and tappet wear. The tappets, in particular, provided their own set of shortcomings. They were hydraulic and had the advantage of not requiring adjustment. The trouble was that a fine filter was an integral part of the system and this required cleaning every 1600 km (1000 miles) to prevent it becoming choked with particles of carbon in the oil. If this regular maintenance was not carried out, the tappets went out of adjustment, became noisy and in some cases jammed, and the valves stuck open. However, to put this problem in perspective, it should be said that by October 1938, by which time 700 Phantom IIIs had been sold, only 27 customers had experienced tappet troubles. Rolls-Royce even experimented successfully with a conventional replacement tappet but it was never adopted.

The Phantom III remained in production until 1939 and when it ceased plans were already well advanced for a rationalized series of Rolls-Royce and Bentley cars that were to see fruition in the post-war years. With the end of the Phantom III went much of Royce's design philosophy: the era of producing cars with a seeming disregard for development costs was over.

TRANS-ATLANTIC TRAUMAS

The production of Rolls-Royces in the United States at Springfield, Massachusetts, was one of those ideas that *should* have worked. The market was surely there, for the booming American economy was, in many respects, a salesman's dream. And unlike most British cars, the 7.4-litre 40/50 was more than able to take those vast transcontinental distances in its stride. Then the company's reputation was riding high, following the performance of Rolls-Royce aero engines during the war, the exploits of those sturdy armoured cars and, above all, that first trans-Atlantic flight in 1919 achieved by Alcock and Brown in a Vickers Vimy powered by a pair of Henry Royce's Eagle aero engines.

Rolls-Royce had from the very outset recognized the enormous market potential of America. Charles Rolls himself took a 20 hp car to New York to win the 1906 Five Miles Silver Trophy for 25 hp cars. He soon became convinced that America would absorb as many 40/50s as Derby could produce, but a far more realistic evaluation of the market potential came from Claude Johnson, following a visit in 1914. Although he found that at the time there were a mere 81 Rolls-Royces in America, it was decided to establish an agency there. This was duly shared between the old-established and respected New York coachbuilding firm of Brewster and Robert Schuette, although exports were soon curtailed by the outbreak of war.

Paradoxically, however, it was the coming of war that fortified Rolls-Royce's connections with the New World. Royce, it will be recalled, had begun designing a range of aero engines in 1914 but it was not until April 1917 that America entered the war. In an attempt to aid the British war effort, the United States government contemplated initiating the manufacture of 1000 Rolls-Royce Falcon aero engines. However, after much discussion, which involved Claude Johnson in a rather lengthy visit, the negotiations came to nothing. What did emerge was a Rolls-Royce office in Cleveland, Ohio. It was run by an astute American lawyer, Kenneth Mackenzie, who suggested a merger

between Rolls-Royce and the luxury car manufacturers Pierce-Arrow, a prospect to which Johnson gave some serious consideration. But like so many such initiatives, the idea was stillborn. Mackenzie's main preoccupation was dealing with those American companies who showed interest in producing aero engine components, with Thomas Nadin and Maurice Olley from Rolls-Royce in Britain there to oversee the work. Parts were certainly produced, although by the time they started to flow across the Atlantic, the war was over.

However, the war had seen the creation of a Rolls-Royce presence, albeit a small one, in America and Johnson was convinced that this toehold was worth developing. A 40/50 actually manufactured in America seemed to make commercial sense because it would then be the right side of the tariff wall; foreign manufacturers were faced with a 33 per cent import duty. Johnson got Royce's approval for the project but the latter felt that, in the first instance, the exercise should be on a small scale.

These certainly were not the sentiments of Aldred and Fuller, a firm of New York investors who expressed an interest in the project. This concern already had large-scale American and Canadian holdings, and a controlling share in the Gillette company. It was under the auspices of Aldred and Fuller that Rolls-Royce of America Inc. was formed on 18 October 1919. The president of the new firm was L. K. Belknap, while the wartime duo of Thomas Nadin and Maurice Olley took up appointments as general superintendent and chief engineer.

The Springfield factory established
From the outset, the Rolls-Royce board in Britain had a controlling interest in the company by holding all the ordinary shares while the preference shares were offered for public subscription. The total capital amounted to $15,000,000. Rolls-Royce of America Inc. was then faced with the task of finding suitable premises for a manufacturing plant. The new corporation was attracted to the town of Springfield, Massachusetts, largely because it was an area considered to have a good labour record and where men were used to precision working: rifle and revolver manufacture was an established local industry. And by deliberately bypassing Detroit, by then the capital of the American

PRECEDING PAGES *A 1927 Phantom I Playboy roadster by Brewster with wings altered for film star Tom Mix in 1932 and appropriately pictured on Mulholland Drive, Hollywood. Provided by Hal Blaine.*

ABOVE *1926 Silver Ghost Stratford convertible by Brewster. The distinctive barrel headlamps and front and rear bumpers identify this Springfield car. Provided by Bob Barrymore.*

LEFT *A 1925 Springfield Silver Ghost. This Derham Opera Coupe is trimmed in sailcloth as the original owner was a yachtsman. A fitted jewel case was used for concealing champagne during the prohibition years. Provided by Cmdr Ray M. Turner USN (Ret).*

RIGHT *1928 Springfield Phantom I with coachwork by Murphy. Provided by William Northrup.*

automobile industry, the prestige of the Rolls-Royce product could be geographically underlined. A factory was soon found in Hendee Street though it was full of war surplus tanks. It had been built by the Hendee Manufacturing Company, the makers of Indian motorcycles, but was later owned by the Wire Wheel Corporation of America.

As Derby was determined that the American-built 40/50 should be in no way inferior to the home-built product, staff was recruited from Britain to hold such influential positions as production manager, pattern shop foreman, plant engineer and chief tool designer. Also, work had quickly gone ahead to equip the factory with an extensive and impressive range of machine tools. Progress was such that on 18 February 1921 the first chassis to be completed left the works. The owner was Wallace Potter, President of the Potter and Johnson Machine Company of Pawtucket, Rhode Island, whose tools were employed in one of the departments in the Springfield plant. Potter then drove the chassis (it is difficult to imagine this happening in England) to the Merrimac Body Company in Merrimac, Massachusetts, where a

fabric saloon body was fitted. But despite the fact that no import duty was paid on the cars, the 40/50 Rolls-Royce was by far the most expensive automobile on the American market. On its announcement in 1921 it sold for $14,500 when fitted with a saloon body, which was more than three times the price of a contemporary straight-eight Cadillac. You could even buy a V12 Packard for a mere $6800. The Pierce-Arrow came nearest in price to the Rolls-Royce, selling for $8550. One feature that the Pierce-Arrow had in common with the 40/50 was that it had been about the last American make to remain wedded to right-hand steering (the last had been built in 1920), and, not surprisingly, the Rolls-Royce was so equipped. In fact, the first 25 Springfield chassis were absolutely identical to their Derby counterparts.

However, right from the start there were some small external differences to be seen. Perhaps the most obvious one was the fashionable and distinctive drum-shaped headlamps which, to British eyes, had a rather cheapening impact. There were other more significant changes in the offing and they are important because they

foreshadowed policy changes at Derby 15 years later. The difficulty concerned the fitting of American electrical accessories, for the Springfield board wanted to use Bijur starters and Bosch magnetos as country-wide spares facilities were available for them, whereas the supply of parts for the Watford magneto and Lucas dynamo fitted to the British 40/50 was virtually non-existent.

Derby therefore sent Ernest Hives, head of the experimental department, to America with an experimental chassis to obtain first-hand experience of local conditions. Before his departure Hives suggested that, if the American components were as good as Springfield maintained, 'we ought undoubtedly to adopt them on all Rolls-Royce cars'.

While in America, Hives visited the Bijur and Bosch works and found both companies amenable to cooperating with Rolls-Royce. They agreed to submit their components to exhaustive testing and comparisons. The Bosch company was particularly helpful and offered to produce magnetos to Springfield specifications and supervision. Apart from anything else the differences in price of the respective components were overwhelming. To have manufactured the Lucas starter at Springfield would have cost $216, compared with $40 for the American equivalent. The Bosch magneto could be supplied for $35, whereas the comparable Watford unit would have cost $57 more. So at a meeting at Springfield early in 1921, Hives committed himself in favour of the Bosch unit and the 26th chassis to leave the Hendee Street works was so equipped. Next to go was the oil reserve tank because the frequency of American service stations rendered it unnecessary. After the 90th chassis had been built, in came the Bijur dynamo to be joined later by a starter motor of the same make. Towards the end of the right-hand-drive 40/50's production life (from chassis 801) the electrical system was switched from 12 to 6 volts, which conformed to American practice. At the time the 40/50 was the only car in the United States to employ a 12-volt system. With the change came Westinghouse starter motors and dynamos.

All these changes were made to the right-hand-drive cars, but the need for a chassis with a left-hand steering box made indisputable marketing sense. Although right-hand drive undoubtedly carried with it some prestige, the practicalities of driving on the right demanded a revised layout, so this was introduced in 1925. This required some mild rejigging of the steering and, so that the rearward exhaust should not collide with it, a one-piece manifold was introduced. Also, and more significantly, the steering switch made the right-hand gear change unworkable, so the opportunity was taken to introduce the more fashionable central gearchange *and* a three-speed gearbox in place of the four-cog unit. Finally, out went the magneto, that very European instrument, to be replaced by the coil, already popular in the United States, where its lower manufacturing costs made it a firm favourite among the automobile manufacturers.

Sales initially got off to a poor start and it soon became clear that the American public did not respond to the British practice of buying a quality car in chassis form and then having it bodied in a style and by a coachbuilder of their own choosing; and with the average completed car costing around $15,000 there was a considerable disincentive to buying a Springfield Rolls-Royce. Consequently, for 1923 the 40/50 was offered with a range of open and closed coachwork, rather in the way that the 20 hp car had been marketed in Britain. This also meant an appreciable price reduction. Models were given such appropriate English names as Pall Mall, Pickwick and Oxford. However, offering a range of standardized bodies meant that a separate coachbuilding department had to be set up at Waltham Avenue, Springfield. The planned production rate of 350 cars a year was achieved in 1923 and 1925, when 365 and 359 cars respectively were manufactured.

The Brewster company purchased
In 1925 Rolls-Royce of America decided to buy Brewster and Co., the New York coachbuilders, who in 1914 had become Rolls-Royce agents. The firm had been founded by James Brewster in New Haven, Connecticut, in 1810. Business prospered during the 19th century with the production of a wide variety of open and closed carriages. Inevitably the company progressed to carriages of the horseless variety and in

A 1925 Silver Ghost with Brewster's Pall Mall coachwork. The Allen manually operated radiator shutters were an optional fitting on Springfield chassis 1-1600. (See also Derham coupe on page 44.) Provided by Michael Gertner.

46

1905 built its first car body on a Delaunay-Belleville chassis. Brewster's first Rolls-Royce was bodied three years later. Unfortunately, in 1915 William Brewster, then head of the company, took the ill-fated step of taking the coachbuilding activities one stage further by producing a car, a luxury town carriage powered by a Knight sleeve-valve engine. It was this automotive detour that was largely responsible for Brewster getting into financial difficulties in the post-war years and it came at a time when Rolls-Royce of America's coachbuilding facilities were being stretched to the limit. The opportunity of buying a reputable, old-established coachbuilder seemed to complement perfectly the firm's chassis production, and in January 1926 Rolls-Royce of America purchased Brewster and Co. for $202,500. From that time Springfield body production was centred on the former Brewster building at Long Island City, New York State, and many of the Waltham Avenue staff were transferred there.

In 1925, the 40/50 was replaced by the New Phantom (retrospectively known as the Phantom I) and again changes were made to the chassis to suit the American requirements. A three-speed gearbox with centrally mounted lever again took the place of the four-speed unit. An undoubted improvement was the introduction of the gearbox-driven mechanical servo that had not appeared on the Springfield 40/50s though it had, of course, featured on the Derby-built cars. There were other minor alterations that had also featured on the Springfield 40/50s, mostly relating to the car's electrical components.

Production initially looked like holding up and in 1927 Springfield produced 340 cars, which was only ten fewer than the projected figure. But from then on it was downhill all the way. Output slumped to 275 in 1928 and in the following year, which also witnessed the Wall Street crash in its latter quarter, 251 cars were produced. If things had gone according to plan the Phantom II would have been produced at Springfield, but clearly the lack of demand did not justify the investment. So the Phantom I continued to be built right up until 1933. From 1930 to 1932 output stood at precisely 100 cars and in 1933, the final year that Springfield produced Rolls-Royces, a mere 41 Phantoms were manufactured. In the 12 years of its existence as a producer of Silver Ghosts and Phantom Is, Springfield built a total of 2990 cars of which 1700 were Ghosts (1100 right-hand drive, 600 left) and 1290 were Phantoms.

In 1934 the company was reorganized and its name changed from Rolls-Royce of America to the Springfield Manufacturing Corporation.

50

The concept of the Brewster town carriage was resurrected, but the bleak financial climate was reflected by the use of a modified Ford V8 chassis. This venture lasted until 1935 and the following year the firm's assets were sold to Dallas E. Winslow of Pierce-Arrow.

What went wrong? Why did the Springfield cars not sell in sufficiently large numbers? For many years it was assumed that the relatively low demand was caused by the American buying public preferring the 'genuine' Derby-built product. Arthur Soutter, who apart from being involved in the Springfield operation has produced a detailed and impressive analysis of the venture, points out that this is manifestly untrue. Certainly 11 Silver Ghosts and 70 Phantom Is were imported into America but in both instances these models incorporated modifications not available on the Springfield cars. The 40/50s, for instance, were fitted with front-wheel brakes, which was something that Springfield did not offer at the time. Subsequently a mere 14 Phantom Is were imported from Britain, which does not suggest that rich Americans were queueing up for Rolls-Royces.

No, the reason for the failure of the operation probably lies more in the economic and emotional temperature that characterized America in the 1920s. For the Rolls-Royce car was as British as the Union Jack, a magnificent creation built with great attention to detail and with a high regard for the individual product. Then that beautifully finished chassis would be clad with coachwork that was a masterpiece of proportion, restraint and refinement. By contrast America in the 1920s shrieked for quantity, novelty and, above all, change. Everything, in fact, that the Silver Ghost and Phantom I Rolls-Royces did *not* represent.

CONTRACTION AND EXPANSION

Royce had been thinking in terms of a smaller car to augment the 40/50 during World War 1 but it was not until 1919 that he got down to the serious business of conceiving a prototype. This was designated Goshawk the following year, in keeping with the company's policy of naming its aero engines and prototype cars after birds of prey. Royce, no doubt influenced by the racing Peugeot of pre-war days, opted for a twin overhead-camshaft engine. It was rated at 21.6hp, about half that of the 40/50, and followed Royce's established preference for six-cylinder engines. However, the project was short lived, probably on the grounds of cost and noise from the upstairs camshafts. (As an aside it is worth noting that in 1913 Rolls-Royce purchased the Peugeot that had won that year's Coupe de l'Auto to give Royce the opportunity of studying its twin cams, four valves per cylinder and hemispherical head. It was sold to Charles Jarrott in October 1914 for £712, at no profit to the company!)

Therefore in 1921, Goshawk II, unlike its predecessor, employed pushrod overhead valves and this prototype car was the subject of a first-rate journalistic scoop by the young Miles Thomas, then working for *The Motor*. This was in September 1921 and, although it was to be another year before the 20hp was officially announced, Thomas was remarkably accurate in his account of the car, except that he referred to its having a four- rather than a six-cylinder engine. It should be said that the production of a four was also considered, with an engine based on the 15.9hp Humber unit and code-named Swallow, but it was not proceeded with. The 20 itself was announced in October 1922 at a chassis price of £1100, which was £750 cheaper than the 40/50's. And unlike the larger car, it was possible to go along to Rolls-Royce's showrooms in London's Conduit Street and, for the first time, buy a Rolls-Royce complete with body, rather than just a chassis which was then completed to the customer's individual requirements. For Johnson had decided to offer the 20 with a standardized range of coachwork, designed in-house by Ivan Evernden and built by Barker. It ranged from a tourer at £1590 to an 'Enclosed Drive Cabriolet' for £1900, which was only £50 more than a complete 40/50 chassis. If, on the other hand, the customer required a coachbuilder and body style of his own choice, he could buy a 20hp chassis in the usual way. But it should be said that Royce looked upon the 20hp purely as a stopgap. He insisted that the model should be dropped when the 40/50 market improved. Stopgap or no, the 20 and its derivatives became increasingly important to Rolls-Royce as the market for the larger and more expensive cars gradually contracted.

The 20 is also interesting because it is possible to trace some of the design influences that manifest themselves in the engine and chassis layout. For it was a much more cost-conscious exercise than the 40/50 had ever been. Royce was undoubtedly familiar with American automotive design, for the 20 clearly reflects this awareness. As far as the engine is concerned, the 20's employment of overhead valves was probably influenced by the American Essex, one of which was certainly at West Wittering in 1921. The fact that the engine and gearbox were mounted in unit saved the expense of a subframe. The Ford Model T had popularized unit construction back in 1908 and the rest of the automobile world had gradually followed suit. But where the 20 really betrayed its trans-Atlantic layout was its centrally mounted gear lever, and it was a three-speed gearbox at that. Now everyone knew that the mass-produced Morris Cowley had a central change (and, incidentally, an American-designed engine) as did the Austin 12, but surely not a Rolls-Royce? For the only 'proper' place was on the *right* of the driver, as on the 40/50 and other expensive makes. Such social considerations resulted in the company bowing to fashionable pressure, and in 1925 the lever was moved to the 'correct' location and an extra cog added, at Johnson's (rather than Royce's) insistence. And then there were those horizontal radiator shutters. Once more, American inspiration is suggested and a visual similarity between the 20 and those fitted on the Hudson Super Six of 1921 is undeniable. But, again, these were destined for change and in 1928 vertical shutters, as fitted to the Phantom I, were adopted. The other noteworthy mechanical modification was the adoption of front wheel brakes and mechanical servo in 1925.

Rolls-Royce's decision to opt for a smaller model was undoubtedly a wise one for, when the 20 ceased production in 1929 and was succeeded by the 20/25, 2940 had been sold, making it the best-selling

PRECEDING PAGES *A 1936 25/30 close-coupled sedanca de ville by Gurney Nutting built for motor agent Raymond Way. Provided by D. Buller-Sinfield.*

RIGHT *The 20th 20hp of 1922, originally an Indian trials car. It was sold by Rolls-Royce (Bombay) Limited to H.H. Maharana of Udaipur. It returned to Britain in 1969 and was restored by the present owner. In all 2940 20hp Rolls-Royces were made. Provided by John Fasal, author of a highly acclaimed book on the 20hp.*

BELOW *A lofty 1929 20hp limousine by Arthur Mulliner, still retaining its British number plates though now resident in California. The vertical radiator slats replaced the original horizontal ones in 1928. Provided by Hy Lesnick.*

20hp (1922-9)	
ENGINE	
Type	Cast-iron monobloc with detachable head, on aluminium crankcase
No. of cylinders	6
Bore/stroke mm	76.2 × 114.3
Displacement cc	3127
Valve operation	Pushrod overhead
Sparkplugs per cyl.	1
Compression ratio	4.6:1
Carburation	Rolls-Royce 2-jet type
DRIVE TRAIN	
Clutch	Single dry plate
Transmission	Integral 3-speed gearbox; (1925) 4-speed, via open propeller shaft, to fully floating rear axle
CHASSIS	
Frame	Channel section
Wheelbase mm	3276
Track mm	1371
Suspension – front	Half elliptic
Suspension – rear	Half elliptic
Brakes	Rear only internal expanding; (1925) front wheel brakes and mechanical servo
Tyre size	32 × 4½
Wheels	Wire
PERFORMANCE	
Maximum speed	105 km/h (65 mph)
Number built	2940

Rolls-Royce model of the decade. But, more significantly, the 1920s saw a consolidation of the company's aero engine interests which were dramatically to overhaul car manufacture in the following years.

Aero engine interests expanded

As we have seen, Rolls-Royce began manufacturing aero engines during World War 1. Output grew to the extent that 2763 engines were produced in 1918, a figure never to be surpassed by the company in the inter-war years. The birds of prey theme had been established with Eagle, Falcon and Hawk, which were wartime projects, to be followed by the Condor, Kestrel, Buzzard, Goshawk, Griffon and, in 1935, the greatest of them all, the Merlin. Its development plays an integral role in Rolls-Royce's, and indeed Britain's fortunes. The story of how the company came to manufacture and develop this legendary engine is well worth recounting.

In 1923 Richard Fairey of the Fairey Aviation Company was much impressed by the Curtiss D12 aero engine used in the winning

American Curtiss in that year's Schneider Trophy competition for seaplanes held at Cowes, Isle of Wight. Fairey subsequently travelled to America and secured the British manufacturing rights for the D12, along with the Reed propeller and various other streamlining aids. Unfortunately for Fairey, the British Directorate of Technical Development refused to support the venture, feeling that British firms should initiate their own designs. But then Lieutenant-Colonel L.F.R. Fell of the Air Ministry persuaded Henry Royce to examine the engine because of the streamlining advantages of its small frontal area. A D12 was stripped down and, inevitably, Royce began improving the design, assisted by A.J. Rowledge, who had joined Rolls-Royce in 1921 from Napier, where he had designed the famous Lion engine. Rowledge thereafter played a leading role in the Curtiss re-think and the outcome was the Rolls-Royce Kestrel.

In 1927, Fell left the Air Ministry and joined Rolls-Royce's London office, where he was responsible for convincing Royce of the wisdom of designing an engine for the prestigious Schneider Trophy. Britain had

ABOVE *The 20/25 model was the best-selling Rolls-Royce to be made between the wars. This is a 1934 car with Fernandez and Darrin drophead coupé body; the hood is in the 'sedanca' position. Provided by Bob Barrymore.*

LEFT *A 1935 20/25 drophead coupé by Thrupp and Maberly. Like the car shown above, it has a three-position hood: completely up, partly raised (as illustrated), and fully lowered. Provided by Bob Barrymore.*

won it in 1927 with a Napier Lion-propelled seaplane and for the 1929 contest the Supermarine S6 all-metal monoplane was powered by a special new Rolls-Royce racing engine, developed from the Kestrel and designated the R type. The result was a victory for the Supermarine seaplane and Royce received a baronetcy in King George V's birthday honours the following year: it was a long-overdue accolade for one of Britain's greatest engineers.

Britain had now won the trophy twice and a third win would mean that the country would hold it in perpetuity. The event was due to take place in 1931 which, unfortunately, coincided with the deepest trough of the world depression, and the government felt unable to support Rolls-Royce further to develop the R type and ensure another British victory. Fortunately, millionairess Lady Lucy Houstan gave Rolls-Royce £100,000 so that the work might continue and the government provided the rest. The R type engine was boosted to even greater power and the resulting Supermarine S6B won the event for the third and final time. As it took place at Calshot on Southampton Water, Royce had watched the 1929 contest on top of a haystack at nearby West Wittering. In 1931 he was unable to leave his bed but could listen to the drone of the seaplanes, stopwatch in hand, as they thundered overhead. Afterwards, Flight Lieutenant G.H. Stainforth raised the World's Speed Record to 655.8 km/h (407.5 mph) in the S6B S 1595. But, even more significantly, from the Supermarine monoplane, designed by R.J. Mitchell, sprang the world's most famous fighter aircraft: the Spitfire. And the engine that powered it was the Rolls-Royce Merlin, derived from the racing R type.

The smaller Rolls-Royces evolve
We should now return to earth and to 1929, the year that saw the appearance of the 20's successor, the 20/25. This was destined to be the most popular Rolls-Royce of the inter-war years with 3827 sold.

The new model was slightly larger in capacity than the old, 3699 instead of 3127 cc, but in general it followed a similar engine and chassis layout to its predecessor. It was also somewhat faster; whereas the 20 had been capable of 96 km/h (60 mph), *The Autocar* timed a 20/25 at just over 120 km/h (75 mph) in 1935. The model lasted until 1936 when it was replaced by the 25/30. Engine capacity was again increased, by enlarging the bore size to 4257 cc. Although the model looked like any other Rolls-Royce, below the surface some significant changes were taking place. Under the bonnet the most obvious difference was the fitting of a Stromberg carburettor. By contrast, the 20/25 had used a Rolls-Royce-designed unit but the Phantom III of the previous year had paved the way in that respect. Not only was the carburettor a proprietary unit but the 25/30 was fitted with SU fuel pumps, Lucas electrics, a Borg and Beck clutch, Marles steering and a Hardy Spicer propeller shaft.

These changes in specification were the result of the Rolls-Royce management beginning to get to grips with the crucial business of manufacturing costs. The whole problem sprang from Royce's fanatical pursuit of perfection. Amazingly, in the 1930s Rolls-Royce was about the only car company in the world to manufacture its own electrical equipment and to produce its own carburettors. This was a reflection of what Arthur Sidgreaves was later to describe as the 'Silver Ghost mentality' and the company tackled the problem soon after Royce's death in 1933.

The following year William Robotham, head of Rolls-Royce's experimental department, made a fact-finding tour of the American automobile industry. He was aware that in some respects Rolls-Royce car manufacture had more in common with the early days of the motor industry than the 1930s, when many luxury car manufacturers were struggling for survival. As a result of his visit Robotham recommended that Rolls-Royce should cease producing its own components and start buying them from the specialist manufacturers.

The 25/30 lasted a mere two years, with 1201 cars produced, and was replaced in 1938 by the Wraith. This used a welded, rather than a riveted chassis, which was a sign of the cost-conscious times, and independent front suspension. This was fitted for the first time on a small Rolls-Royce and was a variation on the system pioneered on the mighty Phantom III. The engine was considerably reworked and lightened. It was a 4157 cc six with an alloy cylinder block and wet liners that again echoed Phantom III practice. But the Wraith was destined for

20/25 hp (1929-36)

ENGINE

Type	Cast-iron monobloc with detachable cylinder head, on aluminium crankcase
No. of cylinders	6
Bore/stroke mm	82.5 × 114.3
Displacement cc	3699
Valve operation	Pushrod overhead
Sparkplugs per cyl.	1
Compression ratio	4.6:1
Carburation	R-R 2-jet type

DRIVE TRAIN

Clutch	Single dry plate
Transmission	Integral 4-speed gearbox

CHASSIS

Frame	Channel section
Wheelbase mm	3276
Track mm	1422
Suspension – front	Half elliptic
Suspension – rear	Half elliptic
Brakes	4-wheel internal expanding with mechanical servo
Tyre size	600 × 19
Wheels	Wire

PERFORMANCE

Maximum speed	118 km/h (73.32 mph)
Acceleration	0-60 mph 31.7 sec
Number built	3827

LEFT *Bought new by A.B. Crookall, of Douglas, Isle of Man, the present owner's grandfather, this 1934 20/25 is a sports saloon by Gurney Nutting. It has covered 90,000 km (56,000 miles) from new. The original colour scheme has been retained. Provided by Brian Crookall.*

RIGHT *This 1930 20/25 was originally fitted with a Barker saloon body but was subsequently re-bodied as this boat-tailed tourer, a style that enjoyed considerable vogue in the 1920s and early 1930s. Chassis number is GDP 14. Provided by Mike Wilkinson.*

BELOW RIGHT *The Wraith was a short-lived model, only in production in 1938-9. This 1939 Wraith is fitted with Park Ward touring limousine coachwork. One of the model's more unusual features were built-in hydraulic jacks, front and rear, actuated by a hand pump under the front passenger's seat. Independent front suspension was again employed. In all, only 491 Wraiths were built. Provided by Howard McCargar.*

PRECEDING PAGES *A 1933 20/25 with saloon coachwork by H.J. Mulliner. This establishment had built bodies for Rolls-Royces from the very earliest days and was particularly renowned in the late 1930s for its distinctive razor-edged saloons. After World War 2 business continued, albeit on a much reduced scale, and in 1959 the firm was taken over by Rolls-Royce. Today the name survives as Mulliner Park Ward, the company's London-based coachbuilding division. Provided by Richard Barton.*

RIGHT *North London coachbuilders Vanden Plas are best known for open tourers, but also produced a few drophead coupés. This is a 1937 25/30 with a completely disappearing hood. Provided by Philip Francis.*

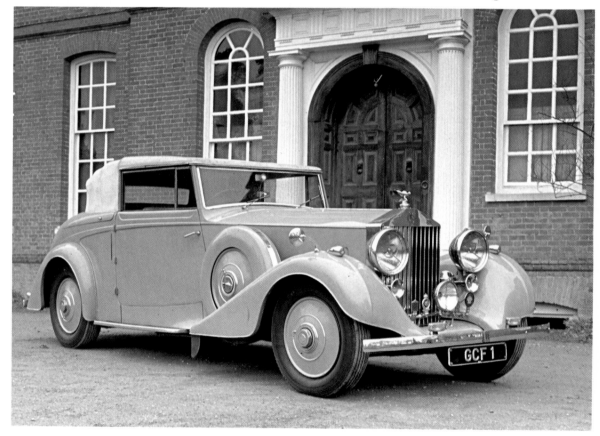

a short production life and it was only manufactured up to 1939 when output was curtailed by the outbreak of World War 2. Just 491 Wraiths were built.

The production of this and the Bentley models was carried on against the background of disappointing sales and there is little doubt that, had Rolls-Royce been solely relying on chassis production, by 1938 its financial position would have been very serious indeed. That year the company's car division accounted for only 4½ per cent of profits, the remaining 95½ being contributed by aero engine output.

A change of coachbuilder

There were also changes taking place on the coachbuilding front. As we have seen, Rolls-Royce only produced its cars in chassis form, and they were then bodied by a specialist coachbuilder. Up until the early 1930s, Barker and Co. was responsible for the bulk of Rolls-Royce bodies and also undertook the company's important prototype work. But Barker failed to think progressively and Royce's body designer Ivan Evernden became increasingly exasperated by the firm's traditional responses. For Barker bodies, though supremely elegant, were becoming

increasingly heavy, and excessive weight is the implacable foe of the chassis designer. Clearly Rolls-Royce had to find another coachbuilder—and did so. Royce, on one of his rare visits to the company's London offices in Conduit Street, spotted a car with coachwork that immediately attracted his eye. What appealed were the light and well-proportioned doors and the slim, elegant pillars on which they hung. Royce immediately sought the identity of the coachbuilder and on his return to West Wittering told Ivan Evernden of his discovery. Evernden was smartly dispatched to Park Ward who had a small factory in the London suburb of Willesden, for this was the firm responsible for the body of the car that Royce had chanced to see.

Unlike Barker, which had been founded in 1703, William Park and Charlie Ward had started their business in 1919 and were undoubtedly more receptive to new ideas. So Park Ward was given the job of producing a body for an experimental Phantom II. Also, in conjunction with Ivan Evernden, the new coachbuilders introduced steel door pillars into their bodies which were lighter, thinner and stronger than the wooden ones they replaced and also improved the driver's visibility. Thus throughout the 1930s, Park Ward's connections with Rolls-Royce were progressively strengthened, and the Willesden firm also bodied the vast majority of Derby-built Bentleys. Unfortunately Park Ward began to experience financial problems to the extent that the firm would probably have closed down in 1938 had not Rolls-Royce stepped in and taken it over. (Barker, it should be said, was absorbed in 1938 by their old rival Hooper, who was in turn bought by Daimler in 1940.)

Derby was by this time pressing ahead with its rationalization programme and the design of a completely new range of engines. It will be recalled that there was no connection between the power units used in the Phantoms and the six fitted in the smaller cars, and this situation was rectified in the new engines. Work began in 1938 and the intention was to produce a power unit in four-, six- and eight-cylinder form. These were to share the same valves, pistons and connecting rods, a crucial cost-saving exercise. They were designated B40, B60 and B80 respectively and had an overhead inlet and side exhaust layout which, by chance, echoed the design of the first Royce car of 1904. The use of a single overhead inlet valve meant that the thin metal bridge between the overhead inlet and exhaust valves, which had proved a limiting factor on the existing engines, could be eliminated. Although one of these B60 engines was used in the prototype Bentley Corniche of 1939 the full effects of this work were not felt until the post-war years.

RENAISSANCE
AND REVIVAL

The rationalization programme for the production of Rolls-Royce cars laid down in the 1930s reached fruition in the post-war years. Before 1945 production amounted to around 1500 chassis per annum. After World War 2, Rolls-Royce and Bentley car output could be numbered in thousands. Undoubtedly the most significant post-war model was the 1966 Silver Shadow, for not only was it the best-selling Rolls-Royce ever, but it was the first one to make significant profits for the company since the 1920s. And with Rolls-Royce Motors cut adrift from its bankrupted aero engine offspring after 1973, the profitable Shadow played a pivotal role in the firm's survival.

But in order to chronicle these post-war years we must first return to those days of the immediate pre-war era when the outbreak of hostilities was looming ever nearer. As noted in the previous chapter, the Rolls-Royce Merlin engine went into production in 1935 and from then on the company's resources were concentrated on progressively increasing its output. This task largely fell on the broad shoulders of Ernest Hives and it was as a result of his untiring efforts that the Merlin engine made such a crucial contribution to the British war effort.

Hives, a native of Reading, Berkshire, was educated at Redlands School in that town and joined Rolls-Royce in 1908. It was Hives who drove from London to Edinburgh in that celebrated 1911 run in a sporting 40/50 and later he became head of the company's experimental department. After Royce's death in 1933, car and aero engine production diverged and Hives devoted his considerable energies to the latter cause. In 1936 he replaced Arthur Wormald as general works manager at Derby and with the outbreak of World War 2 in 1939 car production ceased there for good.

The Royal Air Force's inexhaustible demand for Merlins (it powered the Hurricane and Spitfire fighters) led to the establishment of two further factories for its manufacture. In 1939 the Air Ministry built a new works at Crewe and later the same year another factory was opened at Hillington, Glasgow. Both were administered by Rolls-Royce. Later, in 1941, another factory was established at Urmston, Manchester—but, unlike the Hillington and Crewe plants, Rolls-Royce exercised no control over it, this coming within the orbit of the Ford Motor Company. Also the same year Packard began Merlin production in America.

With aero engine production occupying centre stage, the patterns and tooling for the Rolls-Royce cars were dispersed in and around the Derby area. With an eye to the future, William Robotham and his experimental department collected two complete sets of drawings for Rolls-Royce's post-war programme. One set was sent to Canada for safe keeping, to be followed by two experimental cars, while Robotham deposited the other with a bank in Ashby de la Zouche, about 12 miles from Derby. As it was believed that the Nightingale Road works would become a prime target for the German Luftwaffe, Hives decreed that all the company's technical staff should be moved to villages around Derby, though he remained to occupy the empty executive building throughout the war. So Robotham and his team eventually established themselves in the unlikely surroundings of a disused iron foundry on the southern outskirts of Belper.

The Clan Foundry, as it was called, witnessed the development of the Meteor tank engine, which was derived from the Merlin, and Robotham's excursions into tank design and technology. Not that the

PRECEDING PAGES *One of the rarest Rolls-Royce models (there were only 16), the Phantom IV was only available to royalty and heads of state. The Sheikh of Kuwait was the original owner of this 1956 car. Provided by Merle Norman Classic Beauty Collection.*

development of the next generation of Rolls-Royce cars was overlooked. In 1937 Robotham had been given the task of producing a rationalized range of cars and by 1939 four-, six- and eight-cylinder engines had been manufactured experimentally and tested. The eight-cylinder variant, in particular, saw sterling service during these war years: it was used by the company's transport department for its scattered technical staff. Named Big Bertha, its Evernden-designed seven-seater Park Ward limousine coachwork was removed and replaced by a 14-seater bus body. Bertha covered close on 160,000 km (100,000 miles) before the rear axle pinion gave out.

The six-cylinder engine also had plenty of use. There were a number of experimental Mark V Bentleys fitted with them but wartime constraints prevented Rolls-Royce carrying out long-term testing. So the company cannily lent them to various high-ranking officers and cabinet ministers who then proceeded to do their testing for them! Perhaps the most illustrious of these experimental Mark Vs was a 160 km/h (100 mph) vehicle, suitably dubbed 'Scalded Cat'. It considerably impressed Major-General Charles Dunfee, a member of the General Staff, and later chairman of Vickers, who was on the look-out for a suitable power unit for an armoured personnel carrier. Although this particular project was stillborn the dialogue between Rolls-Royce and the armed services bore fruit and the company's engines were extensively used for military vehicles after the war.

As we have seen, Rolls-Royce had been deeply committed to the V12 liquid-cooled piston aero engine since 1914, but in 1942 Hives negotiated a masterly agreement that was to place the company in the forefront of gas turbine technology: in other words, jet propulsion. At the time the Rover company was undertaking subcontract work for Power Jets at Lutterworth, Leicestershire, where Frank Whittle was spearheading Britain's jet engine programme. Rover was also becoming involved with its own jet development at factories at Bankfield Shed, Barnoldswick in Yorkshire and Waterloo Mill, Clitheroe, Lancashire. Hives knew Rover's Spencer Wilks and after dinner one evening suggested that Rolls-Royce should take over Rover's jet work and in return Rover could have the manufacturing rights and plant of the Meteor tank engine. The far-reaching agreement was to the mutual benefit of both parties for Wilks agreed on the spot. As a result Rolls-Royce took over where Whittle and Rover had left off and the result was the Welland engine which powered the Gloster Meteor of 1944, Britain's first operational jet aircraft. Rover continued to produce the Meteor engine (it powered the best-selling Centurion tank) far into the years of peace.

Although the war years were largely taken up with tank design, towards the end of hostilities Robotham again began to devote himself to getting the post-war range of Rolls-Royces up to scratch. The chassis and engines had been successfully tested and proved, but the problem lay with the production of bodywork. It was an area in which Rolls-Royce had no expertise for, as we have seen, until 1939 the company had only produced its cars in chassis form.

Robotham was convinced that the car division's survival depended on a substantial increase in production and this meant the adoption of machine-made pressed-steel bodywork instead of the handcrafted low-quantity coachwork hitherto employed. This view was confirmed by conversations with Rover's Spencer Wilks (Robotham had even

BELOW *A 1956 long-wheelbase Silver Wraith James Young touring limousine. Just 639 of these longer-chassis cars were produced between 1951 and 1958, compared with 1144 short-wheelbase ones. Provided by Bob Barrymore.*

mooted a far closer association between the two companies). But the high cost of tooling demanded that the company had to produce at least 5000 uniform cars, which in many respects represented the antithesis of the Rolls-Royce formula of exclusiveness, quality and refinement. Robotham, however, commented 'I felt that we had no alternative but to buy these tools or go out of the automobile business' (*Silver Ghosts and Silver Dawn*, Constable, 1970). The tooling was expensive, around £250,000 and, although Hives gave the project his blessing, managing director Arthur Sidgreaves was not so easily won over. He demanded that the Rolls-Royce board should inspect a mock-up of the proposed design. So one was duly created and, although there was some disquiet among board members in response to the rather daring integral headlamps, approval was gained when Robotham pointed out that the tooling was already in an advanced state and, if work on it stopped, Rolls-Royce would lose its place in the Pressed Steel Company's queue. The decision was more than vindicated, for this body, designed by the talented hand of Ivan Evernden, remained in production for nine years as the Mk VI Bentley and the Silver Dawn.

Car production restarted

World War 2 came to an end in 1945 and, once again, Rolls-Royce had made an immeasurable contribution to victory. Not only had more than 166,000 Merlin engines been manufactured by the company and licensees, but others including the larger Griffon had been produced at Derby and, later, Crewe. It was the latter factory that was to be the home of the newly formed motor car division. In May 1945, the month

the war in Europe ended, Sir Arthur Sidgreaves (knighted in 1945), Rolls-Royce's managing director, announced the resumption of car production, although he was privately sceptical of the post-war market for Rolls-Royce cars. Although he made reference to the perpetuation of the pre-war theme, he underlined the benefits of wartime production methods along with a reference to 'standardized *coach*work'. Not *body*work you notice—that had nasty, mass-produced connotations. The following year Ernest Hives took over as managing director. In 1945 Dr Frederick Llewellyn Smith was made a Rolls-Royce director and the car division's general manager. He became its managing director in 1954. Educated at Rochdale High School, Lancashire, and Oxford and Manchester Universities, Llewellyn Smith had joined Rolls-Royce as a technical assistant in 1933. He had achieved international recognition in 1939 when, with Ernest Hives, he had presented a paper entitled 'High Output Aero Engines' to the World Automotive Congress of the Society of Automotive Engineers in New York, for which he was awarded the Manley Memorial Medal for an outstanding contribution to aeronautical science that year. Not unnaturally, the appointment disappointed Robotham, who had nursed the car division along during the war years, and he was given the title of Chief Engineer of Cars. However, in 1949, he was elevated to the

BELOW *The export-orientated Silver Dawn was the Rolls-Royce equivalent of the Bentley Mark VI saloon. This superb example of a 1953 car is pictured in Beverly Hills, California. Provided by Darrell E. and Maybelle Barr.*

Silver Wraith (1946-59)	
ENGINE	
Type	Cast-iron monobloc with aluminium cylinder head
No. of cylinders	6
Bore/stroke mm	88.9 × 114.3; (1951) 92.07 × 114.3; (1955) 95.2 × 114.3
Displacement cc	4257; 4887; 4887
Valve operation	Pushrod overhead inlet; side exhaust
Sparkplugs per cyl.	1
Compression ratio	6.4:1
Carburation	Stromberg downdraught (short), Zenith downdraught (long)
DRIVE TRAIN	
Clutch	Single dry plate
Transmission	Integral 4-speed gearbox; (1952) automatic 4-speed gearbox optional; (1955) standard
CHASSIS	
Frame	Channel section with central cruciform
Wheelbase mm	3225 (short), 3378 (long)
Track – front mm	1473
Track – rear mm	1524 (short), 1625 (long)
Suspension – front	Independent, wishbone and coil spring
Suspension – rear	Half elliptic
Brakes	4-wheel internal expanding with mechanical servo, hydraulic front and mechanical rear
Tyre size	6.50 × 17 (short), 7.50 × 16 (long)
Wheels	Steel disc
PERFORMANCE	
Maximum speed	137 km/h (85 mph)
Acceleration	0-60 mph 24 sec
Number built	1783

LEFT *This magnificent 1951 Silver Wraith Park Ward touring saloon was photographed in Griffith Park, Los Angeles. The famous hilltop Hollywood legend can be seen in the left background of the photograph. Provided by Newton E. Deiter, PhD.*

Rolls-Royce board, becoming general manager of the company's oil engine division the following year. His place at the car division was taken by Harry Grylls.

But this is to anticipate our story because after the end of the war in Europe the Crewe works had to be transformed from an aero engine to a car factory. Output began in 1946; the Mark VI Bentley was produced ahead of the Rolls-Royce mechanical equivalent, the Silver Wraith, the first example leaving the production line on 23 October that year. Although the Bentley was mainly produced with pressed-steel bodywork, the Silver Wraith was offered with a variety of coachbuilt

BELOW RIGHT *Although the Silver Dawn was mostly available in standard saloon form there were some with coachbuilt bodies. This 1954 Dawn, photographed on La Jolla Beach, California, is a drophead coupé by Park Ward. Provided by Bob Barrymore.*

BELOW INSETS *The 1953 Silver Dawn of Darrell E. and Maybelle Barr. The original interior is an impressive feature of this car. Bodywork is by the Pressed Steel Company.*

bodies by in-house Park Ward together with Mulliner and James Young.

Under the bonnet of both cars was a 4.2-litre version of the B60 overhead-inlet/side-exhaust engine developed before the war. Departures from previous practice included a combined block and crankcase casting and *belt-* instead of gear-driven dynamo and water pump. Henry Royce would not have approved! The new chassis was a channel section structure with a strong central cruciform. Coil and wishbone independent front suspension was employed and this demanded hydraulic brakes, the first to be fitted on a Rolls-Royce; the rear ones, however, were mechanically actuated, assistance throughout being maintained by the faithful gearbox-driven servo.

These difficult early post-war years brought a government initiative to encourage the British motor industry to sell its products abroad, thus generating valuable foreign currency. As has already been noted, Rolls-Royce had been selling cars in America since pre-World War 1 days and, although Mark VI Bentley sales there were small, there was clearly a need for a Rolls-Royce version of the Standard Steel Bentley. The result was the export-only Silver Dawn, identical to the Mark VI, apart from that noble radiator. The model is significant because it

signalled the arrival of a common body shell for the Bentley and Rolls-Royce marques. The Silver Dawn became available on the home market late in 1953 and production ceased in 1955.

In 1950 the big car line was re-awakened with the appearance of the 5.6-litre Phantom IV, which was available only to royalty and heads of state. Consequently only 16 were manufactured during the six-year production life. This Phantom had evolved from the wartime Big Bertha prototype. After the war it had had its bus body removed and this was replaced by an open-back low-loading truck body. In this guise Big Bertha was used for transporting car, Merlin and Meteor engines, and at one stage it was charged with speeding. The police maintained that Bertha had attained 145 km/h (90 mph) at the time of apprehension, which the court found difficult to believe of a lorry. Later Bertha had the original limousine body replaced, a much more appropriate attire for a lady of such eminence.

In the latter half of 1951 the Mark VI Bentley and Silver Wraith and Dawn received enlarged 4.5-litre engines, the pressed-steel bodied cars benefiting from a larger boot at the same time. All these models (by then the Bentley was named the R type) ceased production in 1955 and

were replaced by the Rolls-Royce Silver Cloud and Bentley S Series. (It is interesting to note that 'Silver Cloud' along with 'Silver Dawn' had been coined by William Robotham in the 1930s as possible names for what became the Phantom III!)

With the appearance of these new models in 1955 the Bentley and Rolls-Royce marques became ever more closely allied, with only the radiator and badging indicating the different makes. It was still possible, however, for the customer to specify a coachbuilt body on either marque if he so desired. But the standard four-door saloon was again manufactured by Pressed Steel and the styling was the work of a new designer. John Blatchley had been chief draughtsman and designer of the Chelsea-based Gurney Nutting coachbuilding establishment before the war and had joined Rolls-Royce in 1939 at its power plant design office at Hucknall, Nottinghamshire. He transferred to the car division in 1946 and four years later became chief styling engineer. In that capacity he was responsible for the design of all Rolls-Royce bodywork from the Silver Cloud to the Silver Shadow.

The Silver Cloud still retained a chassis. It was a new box section one and was fitted with unequal length coil and wishbone independent front

ABOVE *This 1959 Silver Cloud I is one of the 121 long-wheelbase examples made. The coachwork is a Park Ward touring limousine. It was the last Rolls-Royce model to be six-cylinder powered. Provided by Bob Barrymore.*

RIGHT *A frontal view of the 1956 Phantom IV, originally owned by the Sheikh of Kuwait. It seems he had two of them, one at each end of the 32 km (20 miles) of road his country had at that time! Provided by Merle Norman Classic Beauty Collection.*

suspension. The engine represented the ultimate development of the overhead-inlet/side-exhaust six-cylinder engine. Its capacity was increased to 4887 cc and the new six-port cylinder head was fitted. This larger capacity engine had been foreshadowed in the Bentley Continental of 1954. The more powerful engine was also fitted to the Silver Wraith, which remained available as a coachbuilt option until 1959.

Automatic transmission arrives
A further landmark for Rolls-Royce came with the fitting from the outset of a four-speed General Motors-derived automatic gearbox on the Cloud. This unit had been available on the 4.5-litre export version of the Silver Dawn from 1951 to aid the model's competitiveness on the American market, and was also optional·on examples produced for home consumption from the 1954 season. Similar options were available on the Silver Wraith and the 'box was standardized on that model at the same time as it was fitted to the new Silver Cloud. This car remained in production until 1959, when it was replaced by the Silver Cloud II and Bentley S2 cars. Although externally identical, under the bonnet was a new aluminium wet liner 6.2-litre V8 engine, the finalized designs of which were completed by Charles Jenner shortly before his death. It was Rolls-Royce's first V8 since the short-lived Invisible Engine and Legalimit models of 1905 and its arrival no doubt contributed to the Silver Cloud II being the best-selling of the pre-Silver Shadow range, with a total of 2716 examples sold during its three-year production life. These cars were made until 1962 when they were

Phantom IV (1950-6)

ENGINE		CHASSIS	
Type	Cast-iron monobloc with aluminium cylinder head	Frame	Channel section with central cruciform
No. of cylinders	8	Wheelbase mm	3683
Bore/stroke mm	88.9 × 114.3	Track – front mm	1485
Displacement cc	5675	Track – rear mm	1600
Valve operation	Pushrod overhead inlet; side exhaust	Suspension – front	Independent, wishbone and coil spring
Sparkplugs per cyl.	1	Suspension – rear	Half elliptic
Compression ratio	6.4:1	Brakes	4-wheel internal expanding with mechanical servo, hydraulic front and mechanical rear
Carburation	Stromberg downdraught		
DRIVE TRAIN			
Clutch	Single dry plate	Tyre size	800 × 17
Transmission	Integral 4-speed gearbox	Wheels	Steel disc
		Number built	16

Silver Cloud I (1955-9)	
ENGINE	
Type	Cast-iron monobloc with aluminium cylinder head
No. of cylinders	6
Bore/stroke mm	95.2 × 114.3
Displacement cc	4887 cc
Valve operation	Pushrod overhead; side exhaust
Sparkplugs per cyl.	1
Compression ratio	6.6:1
Carburation	Twin SU
DRIVE TRAIN	
Transmission	Integral 4-speed automatic gearbox with fluid coupling, via two-piece propeller shaft, to semi-floating rear axle
CHASSIS	
Frame	Box section with central cruciform
Wheelbase mm	3124 (short), 3225 (long)
Track – front mm	1473
Track – rear mm	1524
Suspension – front	Independent, unequal length wishbones and coil spring
Suspension – rear	Half elliptic
Brakes	4-wheel internal expanding with mechanical servo, hydraulic front and mechanical rear
Tyre size	8.20 × 15
Wheels	Steel disc
PERFORMANCE	
Maximum speed	171 km/h (106 mph)
Acceleration	0-60 mph 13 sec, standing quarter mile 18.8 sec
Number built	2359

BELOW *For the Rolls-Royce owner with everything: a 1961 Silver Cloud II Mulliner drophead coupé with Radford Countryman conversion. The rear platform is for picnic and spectator sports. The back seat converts into a bed. Provided by Bob Barrymore.*

BOTTOM *1963 V8-engined Silver Cloud III, pictured at Burbank Airport, California. Provided by Merle Norman Classic Beauty Collection.*

replaced by the Silver Cloud III and S3 range, easily identifiable by their horizontally mounted twin headlights. In 1959 the Phantom line was re-activated for general sale by the advent of the V8 engine and a respectable 832 examples were produced before production ceased in 1968. Thus this Phantom V was the best-selling big Rolls-Royce since the days of the Phantom II.

Production of the small quantity limousine Phantom bodies was the responsibility of Rolls-Royce's Park Ward coachbuilding division and in 1959 these facilities were expanded by the purchase of H.J. Mulliner. This company's formation dated back to 1900 when H.J. Mulliner purchased the motor building section of Mulliner London Ltd, created by his cousins at Mulliners of Northampton and A.G. Mulliner of Liverpool. Premises were established in Brook Street, Mayfair, not far from Rolls-Royce's London showrooms in Conduit Street. Not

ABOVE *Unlike the earlier Phantom IV, the V was available for general purchase, and used a V8 of 6230 cc. The example illustrated is a 1966 car with coachwork by James Young. Provided by Merle Norman Classic Beauty Collection.*

surprisingly, bodies by H.J. Mulliner soon found their way on to Rolls-Royce chassis and one of the more sensational offerings was a magnificent two-seater creation for Charles Rolls in 1908, specially tailored for carrying his ballooning equipment. H.J. Mulliner's razor-edge saloons of the 1936-9 era had been much admired, but output dwindled in the post-war years to the extent that an approach was made to Rolls-Royce and a take-over resulted. In 1961 these coachbuilding interests were merged into a single company, H.J. Mulliner, Park Ward Ltd.

But if these developments related to a more traditional aspect of car manufacture, the Silver Shadow (and T Series Bentley) announced for 1966 was a far more progressive offering. Created under Harry Grylls's engineering direction, the Shadow represented three significant firsts for Crewe. Gone was the separate chassis, to be replaced by a monocoque body which was shorter and lower than the Silver Cloud. (This reduced frontal prospect meant that the Rolls-Royce radiator could be reduced in height to return to its finer pre-World War 1 proportions.) Also new was independent rear suspension along with a sophisticated self-levelling system. The drum brakes also departed, along with the gearbox-driven mechanical servo, to be replaced by hydraulic disc brakes all round. The engine was virtually a carry-over from the Silver Cloud III, but with redesigned cylinder heads so that the sparking plugs were more conveniently positioned *above* the exhaust manifolds rather than underneath them. Power-assisted steering had been standard equipment on Rolls-Royces since the Silver Cloud II and the Silver Shadow employed a Saginaw system. Fortunately the Shadow, and its Bentley equivalent, were to prove the most

numerically successful models ever produced by the company and, by the time production ceased in 1980, no fewer than 32,300 examples had been built. About the only other significant change to the Shadow I's specifications came in 1970 when the engine's capacity was increased to 6.7 litres. The model had been refined in 1977 with the appearance of the Silver Shadow II, produced under Engineering Director John Hollings's direction. This boasted the standard fitting of air conditioning and the introduction of rack and pinion power-assisted steering.

Meanwhile variations on the standard four-door saloon soon made their appearances. In the spring of 1966 came a two-door version by Mulliner Park Ward and late in the following year a convertible variant of this model appeared. Both were replaced in March 1971 by the Corniche which, although it shares the Shadow's dimensions, is distinguished by a lower roof line (on the saloon) and a deeper radiator shell. The Silver Wraith name was revived in 1977 for a long-chassis version of the Shadow, which offered a much roomier rear compartment and was perhaps rather more manageable than the contemporary Phantom VI. This Silver Wraith II was lengthened by Mulliner Park Ward.

But the years that embraced the development and launching of the Silver Shadow should be seen against a background of some uncertainty about the future of Rolls-Royce as a car maker. Since the end of World War 2 the company had emerged as one of the world's leading manufacturers of jet engines and, although the car division retained strong emotional links with the aero engine child that had outgrown its parent, a split between the two activities seemed inevitable. This eventually happened but in a way that neither division would have ever dreamed possible.

To see just how this came about we must retrace our steps to the 1950s. It was in 1957 that Lord Hives, who had taken over the chairmanship of Rolls-Royce in 1950, retired. (He had received a richly deserved peerage in that year.) His place was taken by Lord Kindersley, of Lazard Brothers merchant bank, while Denning Pearson, who had joined the company in 1932 and had previously been managing director of the aero engine division, became his deputy. In 1959 in response, it seems, to an initiative by Kindersley, Pearson and

BELOW *This 1977 Phantom VI was originally ordered by Bill Harrah of Reno, Nevada, who created the world's largest automobile collection. Coachwork is by Mulliner Park Ward. Provided by Mike Wilkinson.*

Corniche (1971-)

ENGINE
Type	90° V aluminium block with wet cylinder liners and aluminium cylinder heads
No. of cylinders	8
Bore/stroke mm	104.1 × 99.1
Displacement cc	6750
Valve operation	Pushrod overhead
Sparkplugs per cyl.	1
Compression ratio	9:1
Carburation	Twin SU

DRIVE TRAIN
Transmission	Integral 3-speed automatic gearbox with torque converter, via propeller shaft to hypoid differential

CHASSIS AND BODY
Body type	Integral, with front and rear subframes
Wheelbase mm	3041
Track – front mm	1511
Track – rear mm	1466
Suspension – front	Independent, wishbone and coil spring
Suspension – rear	Independent, single trailing arm and coil spring, also automatic hydraulic height control
Brakes	4-wheel disc, with power assistance from engine-driven hydraulic pump
Tyre size	205 × 15
Wheels	Steel disc

PERFORMANCE
Maximum speed	193 km/h (120 mph)
Acceleration	0-60 mph 9.6 sec, standing quarter mile 17.1 sec

Silver Shadow (1965-77)

ENGINE
Type	90° V aluminium block with wet cylinder liners and aluminium cylinder heads
No. of cylinders	8
Bore/stroke mm	104.1 × 91.4; (1970) 104.1 × 99.1
Displacement cc	6230 (6750)
Valve operation	Pushrod overhead
Sparkplugs per cyl.	1
Compression ratio	9:1
Carburation	Twin SU

DRIVE TRAIN
Transmission	Integral 4-speed automatic gearbox with fluid coupling, (1968) torque converter and 3-speed automatic gearbox, via open propeller shaft to hypoid differential

CHASSIS AND BODY
Body type	Integral, with front and rear subframes
Wheelbase mm	3035
Track mm	1460
Suspension – front	Independent, wishbone and coil spring, also automatic hydraulic height control (deleted 1969)
Suspension – rear	Independent, single trailing arm and coil spring, also automatic hydraulic height control
Brakes	4-wheel disc, with power assistance from engine-driven hydraulic pumps
Tyre size	8.45 × 15
Wheels	Steel disc

PERFORMANCE
Maximum speed	187 km/h (116 mph)
Acceleration	0-60 mph 10.6 sec, standing quarter mile 18.1 sec
Number built	19,412

ABOVE *Soon after the Silver Shadow four-door saloon was announced a two-door version appeared in March 1966, the paintwork and trim being the responsibility of Mulliner Park Ward. This is a 1967 car. Provided by Merle Norman Classic Beauty Collection.*

LEFT *The two-door Silver Shadow saloon and convertible were replaced in 1971 by the Corniche. The high-quality trimming, by Mulliner Park Ward, is readily apparent in this 1979 car. Provided by Kenneth Smith.*

Leyland Motors' Sir Henry Spurrier held talks about a possible merger between Rolls-Royce's car and newly created diesel engine divisions and the Lancashire-based commercial vehicle manufacturer. However, these discussions came to nothing. Then, late in 1961, the idea of an amalgamation between the British Motor Corporation, commercial vehicle makers ACV and Rolls-Royce's car division was considered, but these negotiations also foundered. However, a spin-off was that BMC's 1964 Vanden Plas Princess R used a 3.9-litre Rolls-Royce engine though the 12,000-vehicles-a-year target was never attained. Only 6555 cars were sold before production ceased four years later.

Bankruptcy

These dialogues underline Rolls-Royce's preoccupation with jet engine design and development and in the 1960s the company became deeply involved in the creation of a new generation of 'big thrust' jets. Rolls-Royce also became firmly convinced that its survival should be geared to a successful penetration of the American aviation market. Thus between 1966 and 1968 the company assiduously courted McDonnell Douglas and Lockheed, who were both developing a new generation of multi-engined wide-bodied jet airliners. Rolls-Royce's trump card was its new RB 211 engine then under development. (The RB prefix stands for 'Rolls-Royce Barnoldswick', the ex-Rover plant taken over by the company during the war.) It was reckoned that the 211 was a good two years ahead of its American competitors and was quieter, more powerful, lighter and of simpler construction than the opposition. And, above all, it was substantially cheaper. The price differential was further enhanced by the British devaluation of the pound in 1967. In March of the following year Rolls-Royce signed a 483-page contract with the Lockheed Corporation and the airlines that had ordered the TriStar which would employ the RB 211.

Although on the face of it the deal marked a great technological and marketing breakthrough for Rolls-Royce, there were stormy waters ahead because the RB 211's development costs began a dramatic upward spiral. A crucial factor in this escalation was the engine's carbon fibre Hyfil fan blades. This cheap, stiff and, above all, light material gave Rolls-Royce engineers enormous development problems, with the blades breaking up when hit in flight by birds and an unexpected deterioration in rainwater. Consequently more traditional, but heavier,

titanium blades were developed and this put the engine's weight up, which generated more problems. As costs increased, the British government stepped in with financial support but the aid was conditional on Sir Denning Pearson (knighted 1963), who had taken over from Lord Kindersley as chairman in 1969, stepping down. He was replaced by Lord Cole. But this subsidy only provided a brief breathing space and things were complicated by Lockheed's own financial problems. Matters came to a head on 4 February 1971 when the impossible happened. Rolls-Royce Ltd, after a 65-year life, declared itself bankrupt. Edward Heath's Conservative government had no alternative but to nationalize the company in view of its defence commitments, technological prestige and skilled workforce. E. Rupert Nicholson was appointed receiver by the trustees for the debenture holders and on 23 February a new company, Rolls-Royce (1971) Ltd, was registered. (In 1977 it reverted to Rolls-Royce Ltd.) There is an ironic postscript to this story for in 1981 Lockheed announced that the RB 211-powered TriStar, which first took to the air in 1972, would cease production in 1984. Tragically, the aircraft that led to Rolls-Royce overreaching itself had never made a profit.

Into a new era

The motor car, diesel and Continental light aircraft engine departments were not, however, nationalized. They continued trading under the receivership and in 1973 Rolls-Royce Motors was offered on the London Stock Exchange for public subscription. Since 1971, the car division, as it was then, has had a new managing director in David Plastow, the division's former marketing director.

A new model, the two-door Camargue, arrived in 1975. This time the company had gone to the Italian styling house of Pininfarina, who created a striking two-door saloon based on the Silver Shadow's floorpan. But, above all, the Camargue was offered with air conditioning as standard. The system was the result of eight years' development by Rolls-Royce and, not surprisingly, it made the Camargue the company's most expensive saloon, selling for £32,198 on its announcement.

Not that the big car line should be overlooked. The Phantom VI entered production in 1968. Originally powered by a 6.2-litre V8 engine, its capacity was increased to 6.7 litres (as on the Shadow II) in 1978 for an example produced by the company as a Silver Jubilee gift to Her Majesty the Queen. Also the introduction of a three-speed automatic gearbox meant abandoning the gearbox-driven mechanical brake servo fitted to Rolls-Royces since 1924, which had survived on the Phantom range. All subsequent Phantom VIs have employed this new gearbox and the Shadow II-derived dual-circuit hydraulic brakes, although drums rather than discs are used.

LEFT AND BELOW *The most expensive Rolls-Royce in the current range: the two-door Camargue costing, in 1982, £83,122. Introduced in 1975, the Camargue was styled inside and out by Pininfarina who daringly tilted the famous radiator forward four degrees from the vertical. Fully automatic split-level air conditioning is one of the model's outstanding features. It is mechanically similar to the Silver Shadow, with a 6750 cc V8 engine, automatic transmission, and all independent suspension. Provided by Rolls-Royce Motors Limited.*

Silver Spirit (1980-)				
ENGINE			**CHASSIS AND BODY**	
Type	90° V aluminium block with wet cylinder liners and aluminium heads		Body type	Integral, with front and rear subframes
No. of cylinders	8		Wheelbase mm	3061
Bore/stroke mm	104.1 × 99.1		Track mm	1537
Displacement cc	6750		Suspension – front	Independent, wishbone and coil spring
Valve operation	Pushrod overhead valve		Suspension – rear	Independent, single trailing arm and coil spring and gas strut/damper
Sparkplugs per cyl.	1			
Compression ratio	9:1			
Carburation	Twin SU		Brakes	4-wheel disc
			Tyre size	235/70HR-15
DRIVE TRAIN			Wheels	Steel disc
Transmission	Integral 3-speed automatic gearbox with torque converter, via propeller shaft, to hypoid differential		**PERFORMANCE**	
			Maximum speed	191 km/h (119 mph)
			Acceleration	0-60 mph 10 sec, standing quarter mile 17.1 sec

ABOVE *The current Silver Spirit saloon, introduced for 1981. This, together with the long-wheelbase Silver Spur, is powered by a 6750 cc V8 engine. All-independent suspension is employed. Provided by Rolls-Royce Motors Limited.*

LEFT *The Silver Shadow II was introduced in 1977 and is externally identifiable by its deeper radiator shell and air dam beneath. A 1979 example is shown in the foreground. Behind it is a 1980 Silver Wraith II, the long-wheelbase version of the Shadow, so named in 1977. Provided by Kenneth Smith.*

It was in 1972 that work began on the Silver Shadow's replacement. Not surprisingly, the Shadow's mechanics and floorpan were largely retained and the Silver Spirit, as the new model was called, was announced in October 1980. The four-door saloon was styled in-house and the Bentley equivalent, rather than being given a series letter, as hitherto, carried the name Mulsanne. (This was after the Mulsanne

Straight on the Le Mans circuit, a tribute to the marque's legendary successes there in the 1920s.)

Rolls-Royce's output grew healthier in the 1970s and in 1975 it exceeded 3000 cars a year for the first time. The best year ever was 1978, with 3347 cars manufactured. Then two years later, in 1980, Rolls-Royce Motors' corporate status changed yet again with a merger with the Vickers engineering group. Ironically there had been some discussion between the two companies, along with some other car firms, back in 1917, but on that occasion Claude Johnson had decided that such an amalgamation would not have been in Rolls-Royce's interests. By 1980 it undoubtedly was.

Rolls-Royce can now look forward to a bright, secure future. For the company has successfully made the transition from hand assembling every car to quantity production, if 3000 or so cars a year can be so judged. But above all, every car still represents a tribute to Henry Royce's perfectionist ideals, though tempered by the practicalities of today's economics. Long may they continue to do so.

INDEX

Acknowledgements

The publishers wish to thank the following organizations and individuals for their kind permission to reproduce the photographs in this book: Robert Hunt Library 26; Rolls-Royce Motors Limited Endpapers, 8-9, 10, 13, 14 below, 21 inset; Thomas-Photos, Oxford 14 above

Special photography:
Ian Dawson 24-5, 27, 28-9, 32 above, 36-7, 39-51, 54, 56, 57, 61-75, 78

Chris Linton 1-7, 11, 12-13, 15, 16-17, 18-19, 20-21, 22, 23, 30-31, 32 below, 33, 34, 35, 38-9, 52-3, 55, 58-9, 60, 76-7, 79

In addition, the publishers would like to thank the following for their valuable assistance on this book: The Rolls-Royce Enthusiasts' Club (Lieutenant-Colonel Eric Barrass OBE, Secretary, and Brian Crookall, Chairman); Bob and June Barrymore of La Jolla, California; Kenneth B. Gooding and his staff at the Merle Norman Classic Beauty Collection, Sylmar, California; and John W. Burgess and his staff at the Briggs Cunningham Automotive Museum, Costa Mesa, California. Thanks are also due to the owners who kindly allowed their cars to be photographed, and to Dennis Miller-Williams and Peter Hand of Rolls-Royce Motors Limited for their help and encouragement, and for providing cars for photography.

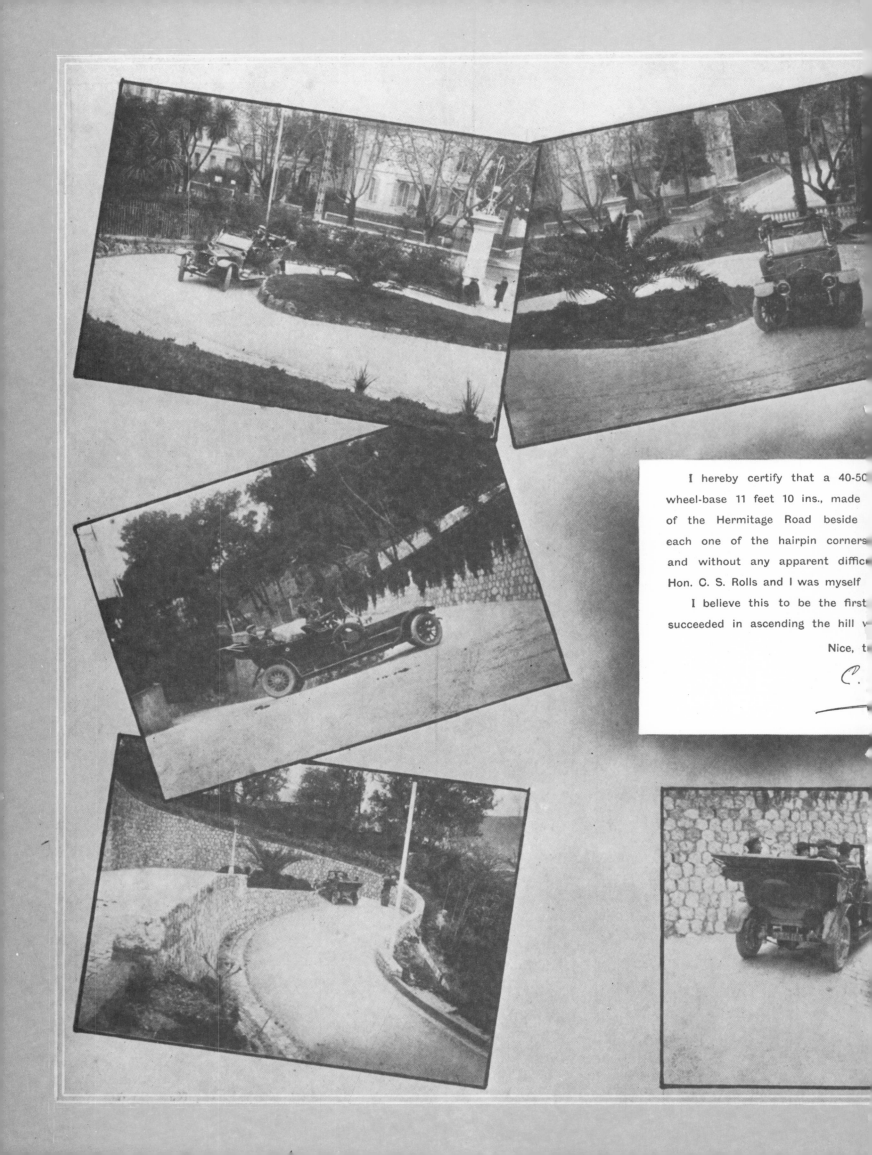

I hereby certify that a 40-50
wheel-base 11 feet 10 ins., made
of the Hermitage Road beside
each one of the hairpin corners
and without any apparent diffic
Hon. C. S. Rolls and I was myself

I believe this to be the first
succeeded in ascending the hill v

Nice, t

C.